LAWPACK

SMALL BUSINESS HANDBOOK

Hugh Williams

Small Business Handbook
by Hugh Williams

First edition 2011
Second edition 2012
Third edition 2015

© Lawpack Publishing 2011, 2012, 2015

Lawpack Publishing Limited
76–89 Alscot Road
London SE1 3AW
www.lawpack.co.uk

All rights reserved
Printed in Great Britain

ISBN: 9781910143155
ebook ISBN: 9781910143162

Parts of this book have been taken from *Buying and Selling a Business* and *Self-Employment Kit*, both by Hugh Williams and published by Lawpack.

Exclusion of Liability and Disclaimer

Contents

About the author

Hugh Williams is a former chartered accountant and the author of many business books. When he was in practice, he won three national awards, including the prestigious Butterworth Tolley award for having the best tax team in a small to medium-sized UK accountancy firm. The other two awards were the *Daily Telegraph* award for customer service – his firm was the first professional business of any discipline to win this award; and the 2020 award for having the most innovative medium-sized accountancy firm in the country.

Hugh has retired from practice and now provides private clients with advice on Inheritance Tax planning and business clients with advice on profit improvement, improved customer care and general business administration. He can be contacted at hugh@hwbts.co.uk.

Introduction

The problem with school is that, while it teaches you a lot about subjects such as geography, history, science, languages and literature, it never teaches you about the important practical things you meet with when you leave school and start to live in the big wide world.

In fact, I'd say school gives a pretty poor preparation for life afterwards.

This failure is mainly explained by the national curriculum not including a whole range of practical subjects, but one imagines that the teachers themselves breathe a sigh of relief when they realise that they don't have to teach these practical subjects that they themselves were never taught, and therefore probably know as little about as their teenage pupils.

What this scenario means is that we all tend to learn about 'life' without instruction. We learn about it through our own trial and error. And for those of us who find ourselves running a business, we have to learn about the business of running a business from first-hand practical experience. This is a pity because it means that we all have to reinvent the wheel.

This is where this book comes in . . .

The purpose of this book's twofold. For those of you going into business on your own for the first time, or maybe those who have been in business for some time, the first purpose of this book is to try to tell you in short easy-to-grasp chapters what you have to know to keep out of trouble. Whether it's a very simple introduction into the generalities of business law, or what you have to know if you are going to employ people, or keep on the right side of the taxman, this handbook should act as a useful tool to help keep you straight and reassure you.

Having just reread that last paragraph, I have to say it made me catch my breath. When you think of the hundreds of thousands of people in business (either on their own account or who find themselves appointed to join management and having to do these 'management things') nearly every single one will never have been taught what they simply must know if they are to do it properly. I find that a staggering thought: that most people in business start off not having a clue how to do the job! Well, this book, in part, is here to help them.

But business is more than obeying the niceties of the law and this is why there is a second purpose to this book: running a business is also about being efficient; about keeping tabs on the finances; about interviewing new employees; keeping employees happy; about selling techniques; and a whole range of issues that nearly all businesspeople encounter from time to time but are unaware that there are guidelines that they might find extremely helpful.

For example, if you have to train someone to undertake a new business technique, have you heard of that simple rhyme: 'I do it normal, I do it slow; we do it together and off you go'? It is such a useful training tool when put into action, particularly for those who have to train someone for the first time in their lives. If you are unfamiliar with training others and do not know about that little ditty, how would you get started?

Or have you heard that wonderful rhyme about marketing: 'He who whispers down a well about the goods he has to sell, never makes as many dollars as he who climbs a tree and hollers'?

So there is a whole host of practical and common sense tips, templates and checklists in this book to help you (and hold your hand, if you like) instead of leaving you having to learn it all yourself from scratch.

In other words, this book tries to go a lot further than describing the essentials of business management. Most books on business management are full of verbiage but have very few templates to show you how you actually go about the tasks they suggest. With this book, and especially when you get to chapter 8, the authors hope that you will find the many tools that have been included really useful for when you find yourself encountering some new and unfamiliar activity as you run your business.

Of course, essential business management techniques are not the whole story. If you run a limited company, or if you want to know how to understand and save tax, or if you want to grow your business, or if you want help with setting the right price: these are huge topics on their own that all require specific learning. We are pleased that Lawpack Publishing has commissioned us to write other companion books in this series that deal with these very issues and which are laid out in easily accessible format for you to get to grips with what you need at one relatively quick glance.

So this particular volume does not pretend to contain everything you need to know about business, but it is intended to cover the essential and common areas with which you either might like help with getting to grips, or which you might like to understand better, so that, at last, you know the key issues of managing a business. At last you can make up for the ground you lost at school when, during a lesson that had, and still has, no interest for you, you were staring out of the window wondering what business life would be like when you left school.

I hope that this book will start to provide some much-needed filling-in of the gaps in our knowledge and which we encounter when we start to run or manage a business.

Finally, if there is anything here that you don't find helpful, or if there is a checklist that's missing and it's one you think we ought to include in a later edition, please let us know. If you send us a tip, template or checklist that we use, you will get a) a mention in the Acknowledgements page and b) a free copy of the next edition. Please email suggestions to editorial@lawpack.co.uk.

Hugh Williams

To my very long-standing friend, Charles Edwards-Collins, who
sparked the original idea for this book.

Thank you, Charles.

Foreword

The four purposes of a business

Before we get started, it would be no bad idea to pause and reflect on why businesses exist and what their purpose is.

This may seem an unnecessary thing to do because most people think that a business is there for one purpose, and one purpose only, namely to make money.

But this is a mistaken view and one we want to put right before we start to go into the whys and wherefores of business management.

Why is it mistaken?

Well, if we were to say to you that we are going into business simply to make money, that stated intention would be unlikely to turn you into a willing customer of our business. We mean, if you were to think that our whole purpose in business is to make as much money as we can from our customers, you would probably, and rightly, regard that attitude as being one of trying to screw as much money out of our customers as they can possibly afford and, no doubt, to their detriment. If that were our attitude, why should you buy from us? If our whole business ethos is one whereby our only interest is to look after ourselves, why would you want to buy from us just to increase our bank account? Why buy from someone who is only thinking of himself and not his customers?

No, this (the desire to make the most amount of money possible) is not the right attitude to have when going into business at all. We have to start from exactly the opposite perspective. We have to put the wishes of the customer first.

If we do that, then profits are sure to follow. In other words, if we start with the interests of the customers last, then success will be unlikely; but the other way around breeds success.

And that success comes from understanding the four purposes of a business.

These four purposes are:

1. Create customers

Even if you have the biggest and most impressive premises in town, a fantastic showroom, great staff and wonderful advertisements, if you have no customers, then, we're sorry, but for all the impressiveness and show of your build-up, you haven't got a business. So customers are the vital thing that has to be created. They are ultimately your only source of cash.

2. Encourage your customers to come and buy from you again

It's all very well winning customers, but if you never see them again, the chances are that any profit you made on their sales will have been lost in the advertising costs you incurred in getting them to come and buy from you in the first place. So, when your customers make a purchase, you have got to make them feel happy so that they will want to call on you again with their credit card handy.

3. Make your customers advocates for your business

If you look after your customers well – so well that they tell their friends about you – the chances are that their friends will come to buy from you too. Customer recommendation is the best possible form of advertising. First of all, if you hear of a friend raving about a product he has bought, there is a high chance that you will think of buying it when you decide you want something similar. Second, there have been no advertising costs incurred in winning such a recommendation.

4. Have fun!

If you fail to get any enjoyment out of your business, what's the point?

Remember that if you get fun from your business, this enthusiasm will spread not just to your employees but also to your customers. Your personal enjoyment and relish for life will become the business's principal ethos and, in turn, it will create a vast reservoir of goodwill and will increase sales as well as the whole value of the business.

So please keep these four purposes at the forefront of everything you do in your business. Put them there right now and never let them fall back into a less prominent position.

CHAPTER 1

Running a business

The basic rules of running a business

If you become or already are running a business, you must realise that you are responsible for your legal and other obligations. You have to realise, for instance, that you are likely to have to pay tax on your profits; so you must keep proper records, which Her Majesty's Revenue & Customs (HMRC) can follow if they decide to check them. It is very important that, once you are self-employed, even if you are still in employment elsewhere at the same time, you must keep careful records and be aware of and properly fulfil your legal responsibilities.

Sales

The most important thing to remember as a self-employed person is that you are not earning money, but selling goods and services. You are not being given a payslip by an employer; instead, you give your client or customer an invoice.

Thus, if you do work for someone you must give him an invoice or other appropriate record setting out what it is that you have sold – it may be hours worked (although charging by the hour can carry the risk that HMRC consider you to be an employee and not self-employed), or goods or services or expenses, and you must keep a copy of that record. If your business consists of running a shop or restaurant, then you should have a till which produces a record of your sales; this record then becomes your record of sales for tax purposes. It is thus vital that you keep a careful and complete tally of all your sales.

Expenses

Whenever you incur expenses in connection with your business, you must always ask for and keep a piece of paper which gives evidence of your expense. If you do not keep a physical record of your expenses, you will probably not be allowed to deduct the expense from your sales when working out your profit.

Choosing a business structure

Going into business is a major decision in life, and before you jump from whatever you are doing at present into self-employment, it is important to choose the right sort of surface to land on.

Sole proprietor/sole trader

The commonest sort of business is a sole proprietor. Its chief features are:

- The businessman or woman trades under his or her own name, or under a trading name.

- The trader keeps his own accounts or employs an accountant and submits financial accounts to HMRC; Lawpack's *Self-Employment Kit* is designed to help such a trader fulfil all these requirements.

- It is essentially a very simple structure to operate.

Partnership

A variation of the sole proprietorship is the partnership. If you have a spouse or friend with whom you wish to be in business association, then a partnership is the commonest sort of business structure for achieving this arrangement. In this instance you should arrange for a solicitor to draw up a partnership deed or you may decide to prepare your own using Lawpack's *Business Partnership Agreement* (available at www.lawpack.co.uk). Not only does this legal document give a proper foundation to this business relationship, but also the deed forms part of the evidence that HMRC requires to satisfy themselves that a partnership is in existence. However, beware of the pitfalls of a partnership – you may be held liable for your partner's debts. Partnerships, like marriage, are not to be entered into lightly.

Limited company

As an alternative to the first two types you might decide to form a limited company. There is one main advantage in doing this, namely that normally your liability is limited to the share capital of the company. In other words, in theory you personally cannot be made bankrupt for the actions of the company. However, if you have given guarantees, or if you have not properly fulfilled your duties as a director, then you certainly can be made to pay for the company's debts.

However, if what you are going to start is only a small concern, you should not normally consider a limited company initially. If your business grows, then there might be tax and other advantages from incorporation. In principle, avoid forming a limited company at the outset, because of the burdensome administration. See Lawpack's *How to Run a Limited Company* book for more information.

Banking arrangements

Very few businesses operate without using a bank account, and it is strongly urged that you open an account if you do not have one already.

Whether you keep two accounts, one for your business and one for private use, is up to you. If you maintain one account only, to be used for both purposes, your accountant will naturally see all the private expenditure which goes through it. You might not want him to be privy to all your private financial affairs. If you keep two accounts, then this problem does not arise, but there is a separate problem – namely you must be very careful to process all your business payments through the business account. If you pay for the odd business bill through your private account, then, unless you tell your accountant about it, he will never pick it up and your accounts and VAT Returns will be inaccurate and there will be a muddle.

On the whole, it is recommended that all sole traders operate a separate business account. Having opened a business account and kept your bank manager abreast of your business performance, he will be a sympathetic ear to talk to if extra finance is required. In general terms, and excluding alternative private sources, banks usually are the cheapest source of credit.

Whom should you contact about your business?

A chartered accountant

He will be the main friend you will have while you are in business, as not only will he help you prepare accounts and Tax Returns, but also he will be abreast of your business affairs, and therefore be knowledgeable about your business, and be a good source of confidential advice and information at times of decision making. Include him and confide in him from the start (if you cannot trust your present accountant then find one you can!) and he will be worth his fees.

Her Majesty's Revenue & Customs (HMRC)

You should contact HMRC (formerly the Inland Revenue) before you begin your business activities or certainly within three months of beginning to trade, or face a £100 fine for failing to do so. The easiest way to do this is to register online at www.hmrc.gov.uk, where you will find you can register as self-employed under 'Self-Employment'. If no mention has been made to them about your business activities, either they will be sending you questionnaires and making enquiries on their own; or, if you fail to make the necessary submissions to them and one day they find out about your business, you will be in their bad books and there may be an HMRC inquiry to answer, with the virtual certainty of penalties and interest being payable on top of the tax and National Insurance liabilities. Once you have made contact with HMRC, either directly yourself or through your accountant, they will be available to give you all sorts of free advice and pamphlets to help you with your business and employment of others.

Each year they will want a Tax Return from you and on this you will have to enter all the details of your self-employed account. Make sure you have a means of keeping together your P60s, mortgage certificates, dividend counterfoils, interest received certificates, capital gains, etc. If you want to prepare your own Tax Return, HMRC will offer a certain amount of help and you can submit it online. However, it is advised that you engage the services of a chartered accountant.

National Insurance

A self-employed person pays 'Class 2' (and at certain levels of profit 'Class 4') National Insurance (NI) Contributions. Having contacted HMRC (see above), you will have to fill in appropriate documents in order to get your NI affairs in order.

Marketing, website and design consultant

Consider marketing, presentation and selling. Your business's name, premises, website and stationery all affect what your potential customers think of you. This is not a legal requirement, but more about how to succeed.

Local authority

Your business, whether you run it from home or from an office, might mean that you have to pay business rates. You may even need planning permission both to operate your business and to display fixed advertisements or signs (including window signs). If you do not clear these matters with the council before you start, there is a danger that you may be prevented from operating once you have begun.

Environmental health department of your local authority

If you run an office, shop or food/catering business (whether from home or not) you should contact your local authority to ask them for a form OSR1 to fill in. There are certain standards of health and safety that apply to this sort of employment and the local environmental health department will advise you appropriately.

Insurance adviser

You will be subject to all sorts of new insurance problems once you are in business, for example public liability, product liability, employer's liability and a good many others. In addition, you might well wish to take advantage of the opportunity you will have of taking out a self-employed pension plan. It is as well to call in your insurance or Financial Services adviser at an early stage to make sure that you are properly covered for all the new insurable liabilities. We are sure David Easdon of Lorica Insurance Brokers, who has written chapter 6 on business insurance will be pleased to hear from you.

www.gov.uk

This overarching public sector information government website, which replaced the many previous individual websites of departments and agencies (such as Business Link), provides business advice free of charge (call the business support helpline on 0845 600 9006 or visit www.gov.uk). It provides help for small businesses in that it is a source of general information for anyone in business. If they do not know the answer to a particular problem, then they will know whom to refer it to. For example, you may want to know what sort of grants are available and www.gov.uk is more than likely to have the answer for whom to contact.

There is one point about grants which is seldom mentioned but which is advisable to consider before applying for one. It is that while grants are certainly attractive, they do sometimes bring with them irritating and long-lasting problems. For example, if you are given a grant to build a workshop, it is quite likely that the necessary paper and general bureaucratic work will result in the building taking longer to put up than it would otherwise. You may also have to conform to certain state regulations which you may feel are unnecessary and on top of this many grants are not grants but loans and they have to be repaid if you sell or lease your business.

Licensing authority

If you are in the retail business, the consumer protection authorities have further regulations that you must comply with. Licences are needed for alcohol sale, market traders, pet shops, food shops, restaurants (both static and mobile) and cosmetic businesses (apply to your local authority environmental health department).

Equally, if you offer credit or lend money, lease, hire or rent out equipment a Consumer Credit Licence is needed. Contact the Office of Fair Trading.

Solicitor

The main point to learn in connection with getting the most from your solicitor or any of your professional advisers is that if you keep them well informed, they will be best able to give advice. So, if you are only just starting up in business, it would not be a bad plan to drop a line to your solicitor telling him of this major new venture on your part.

Publicity

Contact the local radio station, local newspapers, local TV, local magazines and anyone else who might help you promote your business. See also chapter 8 TTC 8.03 on how to draft a Press Release.

Business stationery to be organised

If you are printing business stationery, remember it takes a little time (for a start, it must be properly designed and look professional). It is well to decide what business stationery you need before you start to trade. If you want to generate all your stationery on your own computer, ensure it is properly designed first.

The sort of stationery you should order is:

- **Business letterhead:** This should give your trading name, address, telephone and fax number, website and email address, VAT registration number (if applicable) and the names of the proprietor(s) should also be included unless they are exactly the same as the trading name. You might also include on the letterheading a very brief description of the sort of goods and services you provide.

- **Emails:** Do remember that business emails should always include trading name, address, telephone, etc., so it would be a good idea to prepare a comprehensive email 'signature'.

- **Invoices/bills:** If you are registering for VAT, you are legally bound to include on your invoices your VAT registration number. Consequently, unless you are going to use a computerised invoicing system you are advised to get invoices properly printed with a top and three copies; ask your printer to number them consecutively and put them into either pad or book form. The fact that they are numbered means that there is much less danger that you will lose one as they will all be padded up in numerical order. However, if you are not registering for VAT, you are still advised to get invoices properly designed. The reasons for getting invoices properly printed are:

a) They provide a much-needed and efficient basis for your sales records. If you only keep details on scraps of paper, you are likely to get into a muddle.

b) A printed invoice is a much better advertisement than a page torn out of a duplicate book. If your customers see a well-designed and properly laid out invoice, they are more likely to respect your business efficiency than if all the details are handwritten.

If you run a shop or restaurant with a till that produces till rolls, with all the necessary totals and VAT details, there is no need to get invoices printed. However, only VAT-registered traders may show VAT details on any till rolls they issue.

- **Statements:** Whether or not you get statements printed depends on how many customers you sell to on credit. If you send one or two people an invoice in the post, to be paid at a later date, and one or more of them do not pay up, then you could easily send them one of your normal letterheadings with the statement details printed on it. However, if you are regularly sending out statements to a number of your customers you should seriously consider having printed statements and possibly a computerised sales ledger. As with invoices, if your statements are printed and well laid out, it will be readily apparent to a reluctant debtor that you mean business, and expect to be paid.

- **Remittance advices:** When you pay your bills you do not (or should not) send off the cheque accompanied by the supplier's invoice (remember, you keep the invoice). Normally, you will be paying on an invoice, or on a statement, and will wish to keep the relevant documents for VAT and other purposes. Therefore, you should either send your cheque with a business card or compliment slip, writing the reference numbers, etc. on it so that the recipient can trace the payment, or else you should prepare some remittance advices for your business.

- **Compliment slips/business cards/brochures:** These are always useful for a variety of purposes and are thoroughly recommended. They ought to be properly designed and give the essential information shown in the letterheading.

You may feel that your business is so small that no printed stationery is required. If this is so, then you are strongly advised to record your sales in a duplicate book: your customer gets one copy and you keep the other.

Terms and conditions of sale

When you advertise your products or services (flyer, brochure, shop window, price list), you are inviting your customers to buy. If they accept your price, a contract is made when payment is made; at this point you (and your customer) have made a legal commitment. Except with 'distance selling' (on the internet or digital TV, by mail order, phone or fax, where there is a 'cooling-off' period) this contracted commitment cannot be cancelled without the agreement of both parties.

It's important that all claims you make when selling your goods/services are true. If they are not and the buyer can show that his decision was based on these claims, there could be a claim against you.

There are a lot of rules and regulations that you need to be aware of and it is recommended that you read A Trader's Guide to the Civil Law relating to the sale and supply of goods and services, available from your local Trading Standards Office. Also, a copy of the Unfair Standard Terms available from the Competition and Markets Authority offers lots of useful advice (020 3738 6000; www.gov.uk). We provide sample terms for you to use if you wish in chapter 3 TTC 3.01.

Office equipment

Many people start up in business with no clear idea of what books to buy, what records they have to keep, and no proper method behind their business administration. It is not their fault because, as we say in the Introduction, they have never been taught. This book aims to resolve this lack of information.

If you spend a little time reading this section and use it properly, you will end up with the nucleus of an efficient accounting system that will be an up-to-date source of vital information for the whole life of your business.

Computer or cash book

The best and most traditional way of keeping records for a small business is to use a cash analysis system with lots of columns. This can be kept on a computer spreadsheet or in a book. The 'Analysis of Cash & Cheques Paid Out' document included in our *Self-Employment Kit* provides an ideal template to follow because it is an all-embracing system dealing with both Income Tax and VAT. We provide a version of this in chapter 8 TTC 5.11, but it is far too small for practical purposes. There is a much larger version in the *Self-Employment Kit*.

Off-the-peg computer systems are only any good in the hands of trained users. So, if you are not trained, we don't advise you to waste your money on buying one. We are not the only accountants who groan when we hear a client say, 'My records are all on computer'. This statement is usually the introduction to a mess!

What sort of files?

If you are planning to invoice electronically, you will need to let HMRC know – visit www.hmrc.gov.uk for details. Otherwise, you will need to keep your paper records in files. The best sort of files are A4 'lever arch files'. They are strong, easy to use and will last for many years. It is suggested that you buy six or seven and label them as follows:

1. **'VAT file of sales invoices':*** The first copy of each sales invoice is filed in order of making out – hence, you will have a complete ascending and chronological set of invoices.

2. **'Unpaid sales invoices:*** Second copy sales invoices are filed on this file until they are paid, when they are transferred to (iii).

3. **'Paid sales invoices':** These we suggest are filed chronologically (i.e. as they are paid) with the latest on top.

4. **'Paid purchase invoices'.** These can be filed either by supplier or in order of payment. Filing by supplier (alphabetical order) makes retrieving information much easier for you – and for your accountant!

5. **'Unpaid purchase invoices':** To be transferred to 'Paid Purchase Invoices' following payment.

6. **'Petty cash, receipts and payments:.** It is anticipated that, having a bank account, you will be paying for very few items using petty cash. Therefore, one file should be enough for these for a whole year.

7. **'Till rolls':** If you run a shop, you will have to file these somewhere and a lever arch file or box file will ensure that they are all kept safely.

*These two will not be needed if you are only using a duplicate book to record your sales.

Print and display calculator

Few people think of keeping a 'print and display calculator' in addition to a computer and calculator, but they are highly recommended. As their name suggests, they produce a list of the figures you are adding up. This makes it much easier to check that you have entered all the figures correctly (particularly when more than five figures are involved). In addition, if you are VAT-registered, when you come to add up the sales and VAT figures (i.e. adding up all the figures on the invoices in file 1. above) an add-list forms a vital part of the operation and the list is also considered to be part of the VAT records. You should always pin the add-list to the top of the pile of invoices for that quarter. Once you have got a print and display calculator it will be in constant use for all sorts of accounting purposes.

Till (if this is your selling point)

What else need be said? Are there any shops without a till? Restaurants and hotels are well advised to get one.

CHAPTER 2

Buying a business

Why buy a business rather than set one up from scratch?

The above question must seem such an irritating question to you, especially if you are now a long way down the process of buying a business. But it's one that must be asked. Let's look at the issues.

The famous business guru Tom Peters says that 'It's much easier to start a business from scratch than it is to turn a failing business around'. What he means is that if you buy (what one might call) 'any old business', it will have its problems.

Although you may be buying a business at what appears to be a favourable price, there could well be hang-ups that only come out of the woodwork later. So it may be better to take a longer view and start up a new business doing the same thing. The disadvantages of this are that:

- You won't have any customers to start with.

- You will have to hire fresh and perhaps untrained people, but this can be a great advantage because you can train them from day one to think the same way as you.

- You won't have any income to enjoy for quite some time.

- There will be a lot more to do than simply walk into an existing business that you now own.

But the advantages would be:

- You can design the business your own way, which you can never do with an existing business.

- You can choose the right location to operate from.

- As we say above, you can hire your own people. You can employ people who speak your language and who think like you.

- You won't have to pay for things you don't want, such as an out-of-date computer system or for goodwill, which is represented by a list of customers who, for example, may want to pay rock-bottom prices.

- You won't have to take on a long-serving employee, or a group of them, who have a great deal of influence in the business and who may not buy into your ethos.

- You won't have to go through all the assets and liabilities of the existing business and agree a fair price for them. This can be a nuisance especially when, as we say, you find that you are buying assets that you don't want, but have to pay for.

- You won't be vulnerable to having to pay for hidden liabilities that creep out of the woodwork some months or years after you have bought the business.

The choice is obviously yours but we think it's an issue that you should consider very seriously.

If you do decide to start a business from scratch, then Lawpack's *Self-Employment Kit* (available from www.lawpack.co.uk) will help you deal with the issues that you wouldn't have if you buy an existing business, such as registering for VAT or registering as an employer with Her Majesty's Revenue & Customs.

Should you buy a business in trouble?

It may be hard to see why anyone would want to buy a business that is in trouble but, just because it's in difficulty, this is no reason to dismiss it out of hand. There may be redeeming features that could make it a worthwhile purchase.

But let's start by looking at some of the difficulties and legal pitfalls to be wary of if the business is in financial trouble:

- If you purchase a limited company in financial difficulties and it then goes bust, you are likely to find that you have become liable, in part or in whole, for its debts, even though they were incurred before you bought the company. This, perhaps unexpected, development arises because the company is a separate legal entity. As a separate legal entity it, and not the directors, incurs its own debts. However, the directors are responsible for running the company and if, for whatever reason, the company goes bust, under company law the directors are responsible for settling the company's debts and if the company has no money of its own, and in spite of its limited liability status, the directors may well be called upon to pay for the debts from their own personal funds.

- If you buy a company in financial difficulty and then trade through that company knowing it to be in trouble, you will be responsible for the company's wrongful trading

– and this will put you, too, in the firing line when the court comes looking for those responsible for the company's unpaid debts.

- If the company is in financial difficulty and not paying its debts, or paying them late, its reputation will be very low and this, in itself, will make it difficult for it to trade out of its problems.

- If the company is in financial difficulties, these may reflect:

  a) **Poor management**

  However, just because you buy the company this doesn't mean that you have free rein to sack the employees whom you consider to be underperforming. All employees have considerable legal rights and dismissing employees is a tortuous process and one not to be underestimated.

  b) **Poor book-keeping**

  If the books have been badly kept, the debts may be understated. You may be buying a business that is in a far worse state than the figures you looked at before the business became yours.

Having warned you about these potentially serious problems, what might the advantages be of buying a company in trouble?

- There may be assets you could buy as part of the purchase which you could then sell at an acceptable profit.

- A company in trouble:

  a) should be relatively easy to find. 'Closing Down Sale' signs in a window could be one indicator and licensed insolvency practitioners, lawyers and accountants will have some on their books. The local grapevine will usually be in the know about such businesses;

  b) will allow you, the purchaser, to be in the driving seat;

  c) could be available for purchase after insolvency. So if you offer a price that is rejected and the company then goes into liquidation, you may be well placed to buy it at a lower price from the receiver.

- If you bought the company after liquidation has taken place, it's likely to have had its excessive overheads, inefficiencies or loss-making segments removed by the receiver.

A word of warning

As accountants, we are conscious of many clients who have expressed both interest and enthusiasm for the purchase of certain businesses and have asked us for our views. But when we looked at the figures, which have been presented to the vendor, it became very clear that the business was a sham.

The usual scenario that we have encountered is that the vendor will be hiding some vital figures (key expenditures) from the profit and loss account, so the profitability would be considerably overstated.

The other tell-tale sign that you should be wary of is the vendor who says, 'These accounts are not the real figures – this is what we show the taxman. The sales are considerably higher than shown'. This remark shows that if the vendor is dishonest with the taxman, he is likely to be dishonest with you. He has openly declared his unwillingness to lead an honest life and, for our part, we don't think one should ever buy a business, or indeed anything, from such a person.

This is only a very brief overview of the aspects of buying a business in trouble. However, if you, with your financial advisers, conduct a thorough review of your target business (also covered in this chapter where we look at due diligence, see page 23), you should sufficiently discover the extent of the difficulties to enable you to make a proper informed choice about whether to proceed with the purchase.

What are you buying?

This may seem like an odd question but buying a business isn't like buying a house. A house you buy tends to come with all the bits and pieces that you see when you inspect it, less the furniture. A business consists of lots of different elements and you need to be very clear about what is included in the deal.

We will now list the usual elements that make up a business and try to explain what you should think about in connection with the purchase.

Assets

FREEHOLD PROPERTY

Issues for you to consider: Are you buying the freehold? If so, this purchase will normally be subject to a separate deal from the main purchase of the business.

LEASEHOLD PROPERTY

Issues for you to consider: Do you have to pay for any unexpired term on the lease? How often are the rent reviews? Will the landlord accept you as a replacement tenant? This asset may not be worth anything at all because few leases change hands nowadays for a premium.

PROPERTY IMPROVEMENTS AND FIXTURES AND FITTINGS

Issues for you to consider: These, if they are mentioned in the accounts, can be a bugbear. They are usually not worth the sum mentioned in the accounts because one usually mentally includes them with the property. So be careful not to pay too much for things such as fixtures and fittings.

PLANT AND EQUIPMENT

Issues for you to consider: These will have a value but they are unlikely to be the same as the one in the accounts. We would suggest that you (or a professional valuer) value these assets separately. You don't want to pay for any plant or equipment that you may not need.

MOTORS – COMMERCIAL

Issues for you to consider: See comment immediately above.

MOTORS – PRIVATE VEHICLES

Issues for you to consider: A business owner will normally take his own motor vehicle with him when he sells. So you and he should decide separately from the main deal whether the car is included in the sale.

INVESTMENTS

Issues for you to consider: These are rarely seen in the balance sheet of a business you may be buying. If they do appear, you need to ask whether they come with the sale and if they do, again fix a price separately from the main business.

INTANGIBLE ASSETS, EXCEPT GOODWILL

Issues for you to consider: These assets are also rare. They may be patents or copyrights, etc. Again, if they are included, treat them carefully and separately. Ensure that you understand exactly what you are buying.

GOODWILL

Issues for you to consider: This is an asset that you may not even see on the balance sheet but it could make up the biggest element of the sum you pay to acquire the business. It reflects the sum you have to pay in order to acquire the customers that buy, or may potentially buy, from the business. We've sometimes seen goodwill described as 'the customer list'. It needs very careful consideration and probably some professional help to establish what would be a fair value. We deal with the basics of how to value it later in this chapter.

DEBTORS – SUMS DUE TO THE BUSINESS, USUALLY FROM CUSTOMERS

Issues for you to consider: It's important to establish with the vendor whether he or you will be collecting any sums due from your customers on the day you buy the business. If he is to collect the money, then you don't pay anything for the debtors. If you are to collect it, then you should discount the sum by an agreed percentage (your guess is as good as mine for the amount, but perhaps by ten per cent) so that you pay no more than, and possibly less than, the sum you expect to collect from them.

STOCK

Issues for you to consider: This sum is usually left out of the business valuation and only agreed once the date of sale has been reached and the actual sum of physical stock can be ascertained. As with debtors, it's customary for what you pay for stock to be discounted, and often heavily discounted, because there could well be items that will never sell or items which you no longer wish to sell. So don't overpay for stock on hand at the date you buy.

WORK IN PROGRESS

Issues for you to consider: This sum is rarely found in balance sheets, except those for professional partnerships. It represents the work done for clients at the balance sheet date but which hasn't yet been billed to them. As with stock, it cannot be valued until the date of the changeover and, once it has been valued, it should be heavily discounted because its ultimate value to you is even more of an unknown quantity than stock.

LOANS BY THE BUSINESS

Issues for you to consider: If the business has lent money to anyone, as with debtors, you need to agree with the vendor who is entitled to recover this sum. If it's you, the sum you pay should probably be discounted by a percentage to allow for the fact that you might find the debts difficult to recover.

CASH AND BANK BALANCES, INCLUDING DEPOSIT ACCOUNTS

Issues for you to consider: Again, establish who is to keep the bank and cash balances. Don't pay for anything you are not going to get with the purchase.

Liabilities

The items below should be deducted in arriving at the sum you pay for the business:

CREDITORS – SUMS PAYABLE BY THE BUSINESS, USUALLY TO SUPPLIERS

Issues for you to consider: These items should be treated in a similar way to debtors, but the other way around. If you have to pay the debts that the business has incurred before you become its owner, make sure that what you will have to pay is deducted from the purchase price you pay for the business.

HIRE PURCHASE CREDITORS

Issues for you to consider: The same comments apply to these as apply to normal creditors. Hire purchase normally relates to a specific business asset and if that asset is transferred to you, it would be normal for the hire purchase liability to be transferred as well. However, the liability will have been taken out in the name of the previous owner, and so the finance company should be advised and asked if the liability can be transferred to you.

BANK LOANS AND OVERDRAFTS

Issues for you to consider: As with cash balances, ensure that you establish who is responsible for paying off the bank overdrafts and loans. If it's you, then ensure that the sums due are knocked off the purchase price.

HIDDEN LIABILITIES

Issues for you to consider: These are sums owing by the business that aren't shown on the balance sheet. They could be tax liabilities, leasing commitments or pension commitments that the new owner will be responsible for meeting. You should establish the full nature of these and then get the vendor to sign to the fact that all such liabilities have been notified to you and their treatment after sale has been agreed with you. Having said this, there is usually some sort of hidden liability in every sale and the vendor may have completely and genuinely forgotten about it. When these crop up there usually has to be some sort of negotiation between the parties as to who has to pay it. So be prepared for matters like this to occur, even some months or years after you have bought the business.

OTHER LOANS TO THE BUSINESS

Issues for you to consider: Someone may have lent money in the past to the business you are buying. If he has, ensure that you establish who it is that is responsible for repaying this debt. If it's you, then knock it off the purchase price. If you are due to repay this sum, you should contact the lender to establish exactly what the terms of the loans are (repayment date, rate of interest, dates of repayment).

Details in the balance sheet

Finally, here are three more topics that may be in the balance sheet:

1. **Proprietor's capital:** You will find this in sole traders and partnerships, but you should ignore it. You will not be buying it as it doesn't really exist. It's simply the credit (or in some cases debit) entry that reflects the items that the vendor is selling. If it's a large credit sum, then it will show that the business has been profitable and it may be a good and an encouraging sign for you to buy but, in effect, this capital from your point of view will belong to the vendor. After you have purchased the business, the capital account will become yours and its size will depend on how you manage it. If this confuses you, don't worry as it's confusing – the simplest thing to do is ignore it because you are not buying it.

2. **Share capital:** You will find this in limited company accounts. While you can ignore it for the purposes of valuing what you are buying, as with proprietor's capital, you will become the new owner of the share capital, but the figure associated with this label in the balance sheet is irrelevant. In principle, this sum is more important to the vendor than

the purchaser. If the figure of the share capital is less than you are paying him, then he will have done well out of the sale of his business, which is not to imply that you are paying him too much. If you are paying him less than the share capital, he won't have done well out of the sale but, again, this doesn't imply that you are buying a bargain. We wouldn't get too distracted by this item. If this confuses you, don't worry because it is confusing – the simplest thing to do is ignore it and focus on the assets and liabilities that you are buying.

3. **Accumulated profit and loss balance:** Again, as with the previous point, this is to be found in a limited company's balance sheet. If it confuses you, don't worry as it's confusing – the simplest thing to do is ignore it because you are not buying it. This sum isn't something you are buying, although it's a sum you will inherit in the balance sheet when you become the new owner. However, this sum reflects whether the company has done well since it was first set up, so if it's large, it could be an indicator that you are buying a profitable business. However, it doesn't provide you with a direct measure of how much to pay for the business.

How to value a business

This book won't try to tell you how to value the business that you are considering purchasing. Not only is a valuation of what you are buying, like beauty, in the eye of the beholder, but with a matter as serious as this you really do have to take professional advice.

But you might like some general guidance.

The first rule of thumb, and it's only a general rule and the calculation depends on other factors such as how much the vendor has been paying himself and what assets are for sale, is that a small business is worth three times its net profit. This is a good place to start. So if a business has a profit of £60,000, it might be worth between £150,000 and £200,000.

If you are looking at a limited company and the net profit has been calculated after deducting the proprietor's salary, then this sum should be added to the net profit before it's trebled. This is because, with the selling proprietor no longer working in the business, it's a cost that will no longer be incurred and so you, the incoming proprietor, can reasonably expect to be putting the profit, plus the old proprietor's salary, into your pocket or have it at your disposal.

However, if you don't want to work in the business (and this isn't necessarily a bad thing), then, although the method of working out the valuation is unaffected by this, you have to realise that your return will be the net profit plus the old proprietor's salary less the salary you are going to pay to the manager you will have to appoint to run the business for you.

While this is less likely to happen if you are buying a limited company, do be aware that if you are buying a business where all you see is an extract of the profit and loss account, or maybe a complete profit and loss account, such documents usually hide a whole bunch of lies or omissions. As a chartered accountant who has often been called upon to help a client decide whether or not to buy a business, we very rarely find the profit and loss to be accurately drawn up. Either things like bank interest are left out or understated, or something very significant has been hidden, and it's usually the thing that has been left out that is the reason why the vendor is selling. You should ask a professional accountant how complete he thinks the accounts are.

As we've already mentioned, another observation that crops up depressingly often when talking to a vendor on behalf of a client is that the vendor often says to us, 'Oh, by the way, these are not the correct figures. Most days we take some money in cash which we never write down for personal out-of-pocket expenses. We don't want to pay tax on all our profits, do we?' If you are dealing with such a vendor, drop the proposed purchase at once. If he is lying to the tax authorities, how do you know that he isn't lying to you?

The usual methods of valuation

- **Multiple of net profit:** For example, you might multiply the business profits by, say, three to get to a rough valuation. This is common practice.

- **Assets basis:** In this case you look at the assets that you are going to buy and assess their valuation to you, less any liabilities you will be taking on.

- **Goodwill:** This is a tricky area and you must tread cautiously. You can get a bargain using this method but, in principle, 'caveat emptor' (let the buyer beware). If you are buying goodwill, you are paying the vendor for the capital profit he has created as he built up his business.

  There are three types of goodwill:

  1. **Personal goodwill:** If this goodwill relates to the person (personal goodwill), then it's unlikely to be worth anything to you. In other words, if you are buying a restaurant from a famous chef and he charges you goodwill for it, the moment you take over his skillet as he walks out of the door, any goodwill you have paid for walks out with him.

  2. **Locational goodwill:** If you are buying the goodwill of a business that is close to a car park and are relocating it to a shed in your home in the country, that goodwill will remain with the building by the car park. Again, don't pay for this sort of goodwill if you are going to move the business.

  3. **Intrinsic goodwill:** This is goodwill of a real sort. Let us give you an example of this of which we had personal experience (we will change the details for reasons of confidentiality). We had a client who made the most wonderful cakes. She opened a cake shop under a name that wasn't her own and developed a very good mail order business. She then opened another shop and made frequent appearances on radio and television in connection with baking cakes. As her business grew, she taught

others to bake cakes just like her and she did this to such a great extent that the business no longer needed her there doing anything. So the goodwill attached to the name of the business was intrinsic goodwill and would be of significant value to a would-be purchaser.

- **A customer list** (which is very closely allied to goodwill): In instances where a seller simply wants to get out of his business but retain the property, there may be the possibility for the buyer to purchase the seller's customers. This means that the customer lists needs to be valued; so here is a valuation formula you may find helpful.

First of all, let's assume that you, the buyer, already have a business and you merely wish to acquire more customers to add to your own. So let's focus on the size of the extra gross profit that such sales will create by finding out the value of regular sales.

You do this by starting with the latest figure of gross annual sales (excluding VAT) and then reduce this sum by (say) 30 per cent to account for the defections of customers who won't agree to transfer to the new business. This gives you the annual value of sales that the purchaser would reasonably expect to buy. You then apply the gross profit percentage to this sum.

In case your head is spinning at this stage, let us give you some figures to show you how this may work. However, do remember that we haven't reached the valuation figure yet:

Total sales for the most recent year	500,000
Less extraordinary sales that are unlikely to be repeated	(50,000)
Regular sales for year	450,000
Less anticipated loss due to defections (30%)	135,000
	315,000

We now need to apply the gross profit percentage. This can be found by looking at the most recent accounts.

Take the sales figure from above:	500,000	A
Less the cost of sales (purchases) which let's say was:	(300,000)	
So the gross profit was:	200,000	B
and the gross profit percentage was therefore B/A: 40%		

So we now need to apply this percentage to the sales that the buyer will be acquiring.

So 40% of £315,000 is:	126,000

While you are buying an annual sale figure of £450,000, the annual gross profit you can expect to make from it is £126,000. But you will also have to factor in other costs that you will incur in order to achieve this gross profit. The main extra cost will be production wages, so you will need to reduce your purchase price by a sum that takes account of this factor. You may also incur other costs, such as buying new machinery, but let's keep the sum simple for the sake of this exercise.

Let's say that you need to increase your employment costs by £25,000 in order to achieve the production that will result in these sales. You therefore should take off the £25,000 in order to arrive at a sum of extra net profit that you should enjoy as a result of buying these customers.

And then you should double the resulting sum to give a realistic base for establishing a price to offer for the customer list.

Let's see what this second half of the equation may look like:

You were expecting an extra gross profit of:	126,000
You need to spend more on employment costs of:	(25,000)
The extra net profit that you hope to make each year:	101,000
And to make this sum each year you should expect to pay for two years' worth or	202,000

So, in this instance, you should expect to pay approximately £200,000 in order to acquire £450,000 worth of customers to add to your existing business.

It's also normal to be asked for at least 50 per cent of this sum to be paid upfront.

But after going through this formula with you, will the formula work in your personal circumstance? This question may seem an odd thing to ask. Why, you may enquire, would we give you a formula and then ask if it works in real life? We accept that it's a fair question, but do remember that when a business is being sold or wound down (i.e. closed) or wound back (i.e. reduced in size), the purchaser is likely to find that he can drive a hard bargain. There are unlikely to be numerous would-be buyers about and, if the seller is keen or even desperate to sell or retire, he won't be in a position to demand a generous price. So even if you use the formula, the resulting price may not even reach one year's purchase of the net profit that you hope to make. In the above example, the seller might not receive as much as £100,000.

So, buying a customer base rather than buying a business might be a better way of growing an existing business.

Buying shares in a limited company

The following methods of valuation apply almost exclusively if you are buying shares in a limited company:

- **Share values:** Have there been any recent share transactions that might give you a current idea of how much the shares might be worth?

- **Dividends:** Have any dividends been paid recently on the shares you are buying? If so, such dividends would indicate a rough valuation for the shares. This is a very tricky one to make, and the size of the holding you are buying (assuming you are not buying all the shares) would give an indication of value. For example, we have had a case recently of a lady, who holds a 30 per cent stake in a company and is receiving £75,000 a year in dividends, wanting £1 million for her shares. She didn't sell because the purchaser was only prepared to offer £400,000, so the sale never took place. What this shows is that, without knowing your circumstances, it would be wrong to give you a multiple to apply to past dividends in order to work out a fair price to pay. There are too many beholders wanting to determine a fixed price for beauty. But do take a look in the financial pages at some dividend ratios for companies in similar businesses to give you a rough idea of a suitable multiple to apply.

- **Earnings:** This method is similar to the dividend ratio but in this case it refers to a company's earnings (profits after tax). There is a famous ratio called the 'Price Earnings ratio' (PE ratio). It's calculated by dividing the share price per share by the company's earnings per share. In your case, you will have to work this formula backwards. So if you have a figure of the company's earnings and you divide it by the number of shares you are buying, it will give you earnings per share. You then multiply it by the PE ratio to give you the price per share you might pay. But what PE ratio should you use? Once again, beauty lies in the eye of the beholder: if you take PE ratios in (say) the telecommunications industry (where you might think there would be some consistency), you will find (as we did in September 2006) that they vary between 12 and 78.4, with an average of 35.28. So you will understand why we are loath to give you a PE ratio. However, having said 'loath', we will give you one. If you are a buyer of a small business, you should take no more than 10 (in self-employed businesses we use 3, so 10 may be too high). If you are a seller of a small business, then we would suggest you think of starting at 20. This way you will end up at 15, which sounds about right. But will it sound right to you?

On top of this, investment analysts and the Stock Exchange have all sorts of weird and wonderful measurements of valuing businesses but, in our experience as a professional accountant, we have only ever encountered the ones we have already listed. So we think we can leave (what we call) the theoretical maths to those who deal in that sort of stuff. We have given you what we have seen happen in the real world.

Having said this, there are some specific ratios that are generally used to show you what we mean. If you are considering buying a firm of professional accountants, it's not uncommon for such businesses to be valued at one year's worth of recurring fees. If you want to find out what is the normal multiple to apply in the business you are buying, then we suggest that you approach a local business transfer agent, whom you can find in Yellow Pages or on Google.

But, to conclude all of this, our personal favourite method is to use your 'gut feeling'. If you have seen the asking price, inspected the business, asked all the questions (for these, see below on due diligence); if you know what you are buying and still feel inside that it all makes sense to buy (that you will get a fair or better return for your investment), then surely it's a better guide than any rough and ready formula that we may set out in this book?

Before we close this section, may we give you some personal experience? We have bought a business, an accountancy practice, and our inspiration to buy came from a 'gut feeling moment'. The moment we arrived in reception we were met not by the vendor, but by a smiling man who made a very good impression on us. On seeing him we said instinctively to ourselves, 'If the rest of the employees are as good as him, then this looks very promising'. So the decision to go ahead was based on a very small thing indeed. But that's the truth and it had nothing at all to do with the recurring fees that we purchased.

As to the value we paid, as a professional accountant, we knew full well that such a business is worth roughly the size of its annual fees and this was going to be the maximum we would pay. However, knowing that some of the customers would leave when we took over the company, we struck a bargain with the vendor and paid him 90 per cent of the sum, and he was very happy to accept this price.

So you can see that valuation tends to be a rough and ready business and there are no hard and fast rules.

What is due diligence?

Due diligence is a process that you might undergo if you employ a team of specially qualified accountants to investigate the proposed purchase and give the business a thorough going over. In our view, and especially for a small business, this isn't worth doing – the costs far outweigh the benefit – but you might like to know the kinds of questions these specialists ask and you can find a whole range of them in this section.

Before you turn to the list you may be interested to learn of an experience we had (or observed) when a client employed a specialist firm to conduct one of these exercises.

In this case, although due diligence was carried out, the new owners didn't learn anything that they didn't already know and, a few years later, when there was a significant tax problem that cropped up and which related back to the purchase, there was a huge row between the parties concerned which could only be resolved by a third party knocking heads together. The firm that had carried out the due diligence hadn't uncovered this problem and they were unable to help the purchasers resolve it.

Maybe we are being unfair but this experience made us think that paying for detailed professional due diligence to be carried out isn't worth it. The reporting accountants will wrap themselves up in so many conditions that one can hardly rely on or learn anything new or valuable from their report.

What you need to look at when buying a business

If you, or your advisers, want to ask these questions, we suggest that you write out the ones that apply to your circumstances and send them to the vendor to give him time to dig out the answers for you. If you arrive demanding to see certain documents without warning, it might make the vendor less willing to give you what you want.

Questions with an asterisk (*) relate specifically to limited companies only. Questions with a plus sign (+) mean that you should worry if these answers are unsatisfactory.

1. Why is the business being sold?+

2. Approach Companies House to get copies of the company's latest:*

    a) accounts;

    b) annual return;

    c) register of charges;

    d) Memorandum and Articles of Association.

3. Are the statutory books (which record the names of the shareholders and directors, etc.) up to date?*

4. How and when was the business first set up?

5. When was it incorporated (i.e. how long has it been in existence?)?*

6. What changes in ownership have there been since it was set up?

7. Does it own any subsidiary companies? If the answer is 'yes', and you are buying any of the subsidiaries, then all these questions should be asked of each company being acquired.*

8. What products and services are currently being sold?

9. What future changes in trading are proposed?

10. Who are the main competitors to the business?

11. What difficulties does the business face?+

12. What changes have there been in the type of business that is undertaken?

13. Who are the current:*

    a) owners;

    b) directors;

    c) managing director;

    d) company secretary;

e) significant other members of the management team;

and how many are not remaining?

14. Ask to see the accounts for the past three (possibly five) years.**+**

15. Ask if the accounts you are looking at are the ones that are sent to Her Majesty's Revenue & Customs.**+**

16. Ask to see the latest management accounts for the business.

17. Do the management accounts compare actual performance with either budget expectations or last year's comparatives? The figure without comparatives may be misleading.

18. Are there any graphs showing trends in:

a) sales;

b) gross profit (perhaps ask for gross profit per product, if it's available);

c) employment costs;

d) net profit;

e) cash balances;

f) working capital;

g) interest charges?

19. Are any long-term debts due from customers?**+**

20. What is the company's pricing policy?

21. When did the company institute its last price increase?

22. Who are the firm's chief suppliers?

23. Has the firm had to change its main suppliers lately and, if so, why?

24. Talk to the chief accountant about his view of the business.

25. How accurate is the accounting system?**+**

26. Get the accountant to describe the accounting system to you.

27. Are there any forecasts for future profits (you then compare these forecasts with recent performance to see if they seem to make sense)? If they don't make sense, ask for reasons as to why the future looks different from the past.

28. Who does the firm bank with?

29. Has it changed its bank lately and, if so, why?

30. Ask to see the bank statements for all accounts for the past year.

31. Ask for details of all loans made to the business.

32. Ask for the business's organisation chart.

33. Ask for details of all salaries being paid to existing employees and directors.*

34. Ask to see any standard contracts of employment.

35. Are any key personnel due to retire or take maternity leave?

36. Ask about the pension scheme, if there is one.

37. Are any employees not paid under PAYE?+

38. How up to date is the firm's computer system?

39. How realistic is the stock figure in the balance sheet? Is there much outdated stock still being held? If you are buying old stock, you may never be able to sell it.

40. Is there a plant register (a written record of all the fixed assets owned by the company)?

41. Are there any assets that you see when walking about the premises that are not included in the sale price?+

42. Will any of the plant and equipment that is included in the sale price need replacing soon?

43. What is the firm's policy about company cars?

44. Are there any grants that have been received which might need repaying?

45. What assets are under finance, lease and hire purchase agreements?

46. Are there any patents and trademarks that are being acquired? Ask to see the registration details.

47. If there is any goodwill in the balance sheet, ask how it was valued.

48. If the premises is being sold, is there a recent professional valuation report that can be inspected?

49. If the premises are leased:

a) Look at the lease.

b) Ask if the rent is up to date.

c) Ask what the landlord is like.

d) Will the landlord grant an assignment to you?

e) When is the next rent review?

f) Can the premises be used for any other purpose?

50. Ask to see the firm's insurance policies.

51. Are all the following paid up to date?+

a) Income Tax

    b) Corporation Tax*

    c) VAT

    d) PAYE.

52. Have there been any PAYE or VAT inspections recently? If so, how did they go?

53. Are there any Her Majesty's Revenue & Customs' enquiries underway at present? If so, how are they going?

54. Do the directors pay themselves cheques without operating dividend and salary policies properly (i.e. are they obeying company law or the tax laws)?*+

55. Are the directors' loan accounts overdrawn?*

56. How closely is petty cash controlled?

57. Who are the cheque signatories and how many are required for cheques?

And finally, here is some research you can and should do as you draw near to signing the purchase documents:

58. If goodwill is being purchased, see if the sum being demanded for goodwill bears any relationship to the valuation formula we have given earlier in this chapter.+

59. Is the premises in good condition or will you have to spend a lot renovating it soon?

60. Similarly, do you get a good impression when you walk into the premises? This is key because if you do, then the firm's customers will feel likewise. If you don't, they won't relish the thought of coming to the premises to spend money. Will you have to spend money making the place more customer friendly?+

Ways of paying for the business

There are various ways of paying for a business. Here, in no particular order, are some of them:

- **Use your own money:** This will almost always be the cheapest method.

- **Borrow from a bank:** You can do this by means of an overdraft facility and/or long-term loan.

- **Borrow from another financial institution.**

- **Borrow from the vendor:** It's fairly common for a vendor to let a purchaser pay in easy stages.

- **Venture capital:** This is a specialist form of risk capital with its own venture capital market. On the whole, this form of finance should be avoided because using this form of finance means that you will have to give a significant slice of the action (control) to an outsider. His influence may well prove to be an irritant.

- **Other shareholders or investors:** By this we are thinking of friends or relations who may wish to invest in your business. One point about shares is that if you let an outsider invest in your company, you may think of issuing him with a different sort of share from the shares (usually ordinary shares) that you will be holding. These different kinds may be as follows:

  a) **Non-voting shares:** These can be useful if you want the cash but don't want the investor to tell you how to run the business.

  b) **Preference shares:** These shares usually entitle the holder to a first share of the profits with the balance payable to you.

- **Private lenders:** This is likely to be a more acceptable source of finance because, once you have repaid the loan(s), the lender won't be able to interfere in the running of your business because he won't own any of your business.

- **Sale of assets:** There may be an asset in the business that you could sell.

- **Leasing:** Certain assets can be leased rather than bought outright.

- **Hire purchase:** Like with leasing, certain assets can be bought over a period of years.

- **Earn-out:** The part of the price you pay is dependent on the size of future profits. This way you can defer some of the purchase price.

- **Grants:** There are often government grants available to new or developing businesses. However, grants, while welcome, can bring disadvantages such as:

  a) they may cause delays to the launch while the granting authority processes your claim;

  b) they may come with unwanted conditions;

  c) they may not be grants but loans in disguise and may have to be repaid.

The required legal documents

The legal documents that are needed will depend on what you are buying. In the case of a private sale (from father to son, perhaps) you may feel that no documents at all are needed. But everything should always be done in writing, however informal the transaction may be, and it's always a good idea to take professional advice.

In the case of a sale to an outside purchaser, the following should be considered:

Confidentiality agreement

When you are starting to develop meaningful relationships with a would-be purchaser it would be normal for both sides to sign a confidentiality agreement.

Such an agreement will ensure that, should the deal not proceed, the retreating would-be purchaser will not use any information he has gleaned during the negotiations to the detriment of the rejected vendor.

Heads of agreement

This is the precursor to the final deal and may be drawn up by the parties themselves without resorting to legal advice. A heads of agreement will list things such as:

- A statement that 'X' wishes to buy 'Y'.
- The proposed terms of the deal, the price and what is being bought for that price. The vendor and purchaser create these terms.
- The timetable.
- The price.
- Who will manage the business before the deal is signed?
- Who will pay the legal fees?

Deed of sale (contract)

If you are buying from a stranger, it would be risky not to have a legal document drawn up itemising exactly what you are buying. Many of the conditions will be standard and are summed up in a document known as a TUPE, which stands for 'Transfer of an Undertaking and Protection of Employment'.

The usual clauses in such a contract are as follows (we apologise for using legal terms that mean little to a layperson but they are what you will have to deal with):

- Parties to the deal
- Definitions and interpretations
- Conditions
- Sale and purchase
- Consideration
- Period before completion

- Warranties and indemnity

- Restrictions on the vendors

- Pensions

- Confidentiality

- General

- Notices

- Governing law

- Supporting schedules – do leave this to the professional.

Please note that, under TUPE, when you buy a business the employees who arrive with that business bring with them all their rights from the previous employment. So, for example, if someone had been employed by the previous business for many years and a year after you buy it you want to make him redundant, his redundancy entitlement will be calculated on all of his years of employment and not just the one year for which you have been paying his wages. For more information on employment law, see Lawpack's *Employment Law Made Easy* book (available from www.lawpack.co.uk).

Lease

If you are renting premises, there will be a lease to consider and you will have to obtain the advice of a solicitor for such a matter.

Contract for property purchase

If you are buying the property, then there will be a contract for that. Again, a solicitor will be required.

Employment contracts

You should draw up employment contracts for all the employees that you will be taking on.

There may also be other legal documents that establish the business relationship between you and your co-owners, such as:

- a partnership deed, which lays down the legal agreements between the partners on how the business is to be run;

- a shareholders' agreement, which lays down the legal agreements between the shareholders on how the business is to be run; and/or

- a director's service contract, which is a director's contract of employment with the company.

Making sure that the business doesn't die the day you take it over

There is a great danger when you buy a business and the former owner disappears that the business may die. As with heads of businesses, it's the same with hearts; when they are transplanted the new heart tends to be rejected. So you need to counteract this danger by taking specific action to win the hearts and minds of the employees; and you should think seriously about doing this before you walk into the business on day one.

Here are some ideas that we've tried out and we believe that they all work well:

The importance of a mission statement

The concept of a mission statement has been downgraded ever since it was introduced. People tend to miss the point of a mission statement but they are also missing an opportunity.

For so many people, coming to work is a chore. It's a way of making enough money to subsist; to them, the existence of the job and the pay packet is all that matters. What if things could be different?

Imagine a business where the employees come to work each day with a spring in their step, wanting to really enjoy the hours they will spend at work that day and who are determined to serve their customers as well as they possibly can. Such employees will be helping to create more customers; more customers mean more sales; more sales mean more profits and more profits mean more money for those who work in the business.

Whenever we, in our accountancy practice, find that a client has shown us a spontaneous show of gratitude for our work (we call such gestures 'wows'), it makes us all feel great; in the exact opposite way that a moaning client can really put the dampeners on the day.

So if you run a business where the customers are often saying 'Wow, what you do is really great', that in itself must make it a great place to work.

What you need to do, therefore, is create a climate where the employees are forever trying to make the clients go 'wow'. To get your new employees (the ones you are taking over with the business) to adopt this philosophy you probably need to take them away for a half-day (perhaps a full day) and ask them the questions that are included in a mini-planning session (see chapter 8) to see if you can find a mission statement that encapsulates this philosophy.

Let us tell you how we do it in our business. Our firm occasionally ask our clients to rate us by giving us a score out of ten for how well we are looking after them. This has proved to be an extremely neat idea because it has led us to formulate our own mission statement, which reads, 'We want to score ten out of ten in everything we do for our clients'.

It's very short – so it's memorable – and it heads up all of the firm's employment contracts. In other words, it's the first thing an employee reads when he gets his contract each year and so it focuses (or is intended to focus) his mind on what he comes to work for.

Could you do the same in your business? (Please feel free to crib from our mission statement.) If you can, we think you will be very pleasantly surprised by your employees' positive opinions of you and their whole job.

Looking after the employees you take over

1. Give them a pay rise on day one. This is a great way for them to take to you – the new management. They will have grown used to their former employer and will view you with suspicion, so if you start by showing just how much you value them and want them to keep doing the work that has made the business into one that you have decided to buy, this will get them onside right from the start.

2. Ask them to complete a questionnaire with questions such as:

    a) Are you happy in your job?

    b) If not, what can we do to make it better for you?

    c) What kind of work do you like doing?

    d) What kind of work do you not like doing?

    e) Who is your favourite client?

    f) Who is your least favourite client?

    g) Should we be asking this client to take his business elsewhere?

    h) What skills would you like to learn?

    i) When would you like to retire or how long are you planning to work with us?

    j) What could we do to make your working life better?

3. Ask them to prepare a job description of their own jobs. That way you'll know what they do each day.

4. Invite them to a mini-planning session.

5. If they haven't got a contract of employment, then ensure that they get one as soon as possible.

6. Give them benefits that they may not be already receiving such as:

a) a pension scheme;

b) private medical health insurance;

c) death in service benefits so that if they die while working for you, their family will be paid some money; and

d) permanent health insurance.

7. Give them the freedom to do their jobs to the best of their ability. Each of your employees will know far more about their job than you ever will, so respect them for that and never try to learn to do it yourself. Delegate as much as you possibly can and don't continually check up on them. Instead, help them to achieve for themselves and your customers as much as they possibly can. Tell them that your job is simply to manage the business and to try to make them as happy and as fulfilled as possible. If, instead of delegating as much as you possibly can to them, you watch over them and interrupt their day with unhelpful remarks, they will grow weary and probably leave. The departure of staff will ensure that the business stagnates and eventually dies.

Looking after existing customers

The last thing you want when you buy a business is for the customers to go and take their custom elsewhere. So how do you stop them?

We bought another business and managed to keep the vast majority of them, so here are the details of how we ensured their loyalty:

1. We sent them all a newsletter introducing ourselves and trying to get across the notion that our job was to make their lives better.

2. Because the business that we bought used a billing philosophy that we had rejected, we needed to tell our new customers that there would be changes made in 12 months' time. These changes would be explained to them (and the benefits that they would enjoy as a result) in such a way that if they didn't like what was proposed, they were free to take their business elsewhere.

3. We did a number of things in the business that needed doing. Email hadn't really got going at that time and the previous owner had decided that because he was selling, he didn't want to spend money on getting the photocopier mended or buying a fax machine. These two things were put right at a very early stage and email was introduced. Although these changes may sound very mundane, we were impressed by how much the customers noticed the improvements and congratulated us on carrying them out.

On the whole, it's important that you tell the customers that you have arrived and that your main aim in life is to make them happy.

Creating an action plan for the business

If a strategic plan is to work, you have to get your employees to help you make it. If you just present it to them and tell them to get on with it, they will never own it and you will have wasted your time and money.

Set aside some time during the week (not at a weekend or in the evening) to take a long hard look at the business and, after you and your employees have taken stock, decide where you all want it to head.

To assist you, you can hold a mini-planning session (see chapter 8), which is basically an agenda for a day (or at least half a day) away with your people. You should give each of your employees a copy to ponder before you all assemble and start asking around for answers to these key questions. You will be amazed by the excitement this process produces.

However, you should be aware that you need to get this meeting underway at an early stage. If you leave it for a year, and give the business time for your personal weaknesses to get established, you could find that a mini-planning session becomes quite uncomfortable for you because, if you have been in charge for more than a few months, some of the weaknesses will be due to you.

So hold this meeting as soon as possible and then all the failures can be fairly attributed to the previous owner and not to you!

If you haven't already done so:

1. Look at the checklist for holding a mini-planning session.

2. Type it out (or your version of it).

3. Fix a time and place for your key people to meet up away from your place of business.

4. Then simply make sure that they all turn up!

But before arranging this meeting, do think about what you want the end result of the day to be. In our view, you want to have created a very simple action plan that looks like the example in chapter 8 TTC 5.04.

Creating your vision for the business

There is one vital ingredient that we've left out. It's the one that holds it all together and, now that you have bedded yourself into this new business, it's the one you can start to address seriously. It's writing an answer to that question you will have been asking yourself, 'What do I plan to get out of this business that I have purchased?'

The simple answer given by author Michael Gerber, who wrote *The E-Myth*, to this question is 'to sell it'. So, following the Gerber principle, now that you have bought the business you had better make some realistic plans to sell it.

Don't panic, however. This doesn't mean that you must plan to sell it tomorrow, but one day you should plan to sell it, or at least retire, and let it pay you a dividend while you do something else. So your vision statement should read something like this:

'I'm trying to manage this business so that in ten years' time it becomes known as the best in the neighbourhood, where my employees will be proud to come to work and be well paid for their contribution and where their overriding aim is to serve the customers as well as or better than they themselves would like to be treated.

I will be free to work as much or as little as I want in the firm so that, if I want to, I can sell it for £X or expect to receive an annual income from it of £Y.'

As we have seen, if you want to calculate what X and Y might amount to, you take the present profits of the business; envisage how much you expect them to grow in the next (say) ten years and that will give you Y. To get to X, you simply multiply Y by 3.

This may seem absurdly simple but it's the only way to do business. If you can remember it and visualise it, then you have a clear target to aim for. If it's contained in a report which is three centimetres thick, you'll read it once, never look at it again and forget what it says.

Making a business plan

It would be strange in a book of this nature not to mention what a business plan might look like. Please note that a business plan is not an action plan. A business plan might be needed if you are seeking an outside investor, bank finance or perhaps applying for Investors in People status (a framework for a business's improvement through its people).

Here is a list of suggested contents for such a business plan:

BUSINESS PROFILE

- **Business overview and mission statement**

  Provide a general outline of your business, so that outsiders will understand what your business is all about.

- **Unique features**

  Discuss the advantage that gives you the edge in the market. What are you doing that others aren't?

- **Sales overview**

  Show in tabular form your recent sales figures.

- **Sales forecast**

  Show projected sales and profits for the next three years.

- **Proof of sales**

  Show some evidence that your projections will come to fruition.

COMPETITIVE PROFILE

- **Market size**

  What is the total market and is it growing?

- **Market segments**

  Try to break the market down into smaller segments and show how your product fits into that segment.

- **Market trends**

  Show what is happening to your market that will affect your business.

- **Competitive analysis**

  How do you compare with your competitors?

STRATEGIC DIRECTION

- **SWOT analysis**

  Write down in four tables your strengths, weaknesses, opportunities and threats.

- **Vision statement**

  This is a concise statement of where you want to be in three, five and ten years' time.

- **Target market**

  Give examples of to whom exactly you will be selling your products and services.

- **Positioning**

  How will you position your products? Is there a gap in the market? What benefits will you be selling?

- **Strategy highlights**

  What are the major things you will need in order to achieve your financial targets?

- **Investor information**

  What do you want to borrow and what return on their investment can your investors expect?

THE ACTUAL PLAN

- **Business objectives**

  You simply state, 'We want to sell £X,000 per year at a gross profit of Y per cent, resulting in a net profit of Z per cent.'

- **Marketing plan**

  In detail, with costs and timescale, how are you going to market your product?

THE ACTUAL PLAN (CONTINUED)

- **Financial plan**

  In summary, how and when is the money going to come in and out? Use a simple spreadsheet including the details in the next section.

- **Organisational plan**

  In detail, who is going to do what and when?

- **Any other plans**

  Include any other relevant plans you have (including your current action plan).

FINANCIALS

- **First-year budget**

  This is where your accountant can really help.

- **First-year cash flow**

  See above.

- **Five-year budget**

  See above.

- **Five-year sales forecast**

  See above.

- **Five-year balance sheets**

  See above.

IMPLEMENTATION

This section should only be completed when the business has something to report. It can be ignored if the business has not yet started.

- **Milestones**

  A list of who is going to do what and when and, importantly, a record of whether this has been done.

- **Actual**

  A comparison of budgets with actual performance.

CHAPTER 3

Business law

Everyone is subject to the laws of the land and businesspeople are no exception. There is a wealth of law to which they are subject and yet many businesspeople are blissfully unaware of the range of laws that they must obey.

To try to rectify this lapse, let's begin with a list of some of the more important types of law that affect businesses. Collectively these are known as Business Law or Commercial Law:

- Anti-trust
- Bankruptcy – insolvency
- Bribery Act
- Company law
- Consumer credit
- Consumer protection (see Product Liability below)
- Law of contract
- Cyber law
- Data protection
- Employment law including tax law on paying wages
- Equal opportunities
- Estoppel
- Fraud
- Health and safety
- Intellectual property law

  a) Copyright

  b) Patent

  c) Trade secret

d) Trade

- International trade law
- Non-disclosure agreement
- Partnership law
- Product liability
- Property law
- Sale of Goods Act
- Tax law
- Torts

We will now give the briefest of overviews for each of the above. Suffice it to say that, if you think you may have suffered from another person or business breaking any of the following, or even fear that you may be guilty of breaking one yourself, you should take legal advice without delay.

Anti-trust laws

These laws prohibit anticompetitive behaviour and unfair business practices.

Bankruptcy – insolvency

Owners and directors of businesses that trade while insolvent (i.e. unable to pay their debts) are breaking the law. Even if they think they are protected by limited liability, that is no excuse for reckless or irresponsible behaviour in business and, if a judge considers that a director has been trading while unable to pay his debts, that judge is likely to look to the directors to settle the debts out of their own private pockets.

Bribery Act

The crime of bribery covers both bribing and being bribed. Bribery is when a person offers, gives or promises to give a financial or other advantage to another individual in exchange for improperly performing a relevant function or activity.

Being bribed means requesting, or accepting, an advantage, in exchange for improperly performing such a function or activity.

Financial or other advantage includes contracts, non-monetary gifts and offers of employment.

The most concerning part of this legislation is the definition of 'relevant function or activity' because it is extremely far reaching. It covers 'any function of a public nature; any activity connected with a business, trade or profession; any activity performed in the course of a person's employment; or any activity performed by or on behalf of a body of persons whether corporate or unincorporated'. In addition, it applies to both private and public industry, and even encompasses activities performed outside the UK, to the effect that a French business with branches in the UK and which pays a bribe in Germany, could actually face prosecution in the UK.

The activity will be considered to be 'improperly' performed when what would be expected to be when the normal expectation of good faith has been broken, or when something has been carried out in a way not expected of a person in a position of trust.

The standard in deciding what would be expected is what a reasonable person in the UK might expect of a person in such a position. In other words, being offered reasonable hospitality by a client is unlikely to be regarded as a bribe!

The far reaching nature of this law can be seen in the fact that, where a bribe has been given outside the UK, local customs should be ignored, unless they form part of the established law of that country.

Bribery of foreign public officials is now a distinct crime. A person will be guilty of bribery if he bribes a foreign public official, even through a third party or go-between. That said, and this may seem contrary to the draconian spirit of the law, the bribe will be permissible if the established law of the country concerned allows an official to accept it.

All businesses are now required to have specific policies and procedures to prevent bribery on their behalf. (You will notice that we make reference to what these might be in the sample 'terms of employment'.)

This is because a commercial organisation can be guilty of bribery if it is carried out by an employee, an agent, a subsidiary, or even another thirdparty.

The commercial organisation might be let off, if it can show that, it had adequate procedures designed to their employees and associates offering or accepting bribes. That said, the burden of proof will be on the commercial organisation to prove that they had adequate policies in place and which they could show that they had consistently tried to put into effect with the people concerned.

Company law

Company law is the law that affects limited companies. This law only affects limited companies and is the subject of our special guide *How to Run a Limited Company*.

Consumer credit

This is a little known area of the law and yet it appears to be extremely important. What the Office of Fair Trading and the Consumer Credit Act say is that, if you sell goods or services on credit, you are likely to need a consumer credit licence. Some traders are covered by a group licence and do not have to register individually (e.g. chartered accountants do not have to register because they are covered by a group licence taken out by their institute), but if you are not so covered, then this is an area you should investigate.

You will not need a licence if you simply accept cash, cheques and credit cards, nor will you need one if you allow your customers to pay their bills in four or fewer instalments within a year beginning with the date of the agreement. But most businesses, it seems, should register but, on wonders, have the – are they, breaking, the law, albeit inadvertently?

A licence costs over £500 for a sole trader; double that for a partnership and more for larger organisations. The licence lasts indefinitely but there are maintenance fees payable and for details of these, and all aspects of this particular law, you should ask the Office of Fair Trading.

Law of contract

Whether you buy or sell products or services, both parties are subject to the law of contract. In short the seller is legally obliged to provide the goods or services requested and at the price specified. The buyer is obliged to pay for the goods or services in line with the terms offered by the seller.

This is, not unexpectedly, a huge subject. It covers all sorts of things like 'terms of business' and guarantees, as well as resultant court procedures. In short every business should have clearly written and published terms of business available for any buyer to read. If they don't, they may find it more difficult to claim payment if the buyer fails to pay. While the most famous maxim 'caveat emptor' (let the buyer beware) appears to protect the supplier, modern contract law tends to favour the buyer and all businesspeople should be aware of this.

We provide some suggested terms of business in chapter 8.

Cyber law

It would be a brave author who pretended that he knew the full gamut of cyber law and it would be a brave publisher who sells a book that pretends to give an up-to-date picture of where this special area of the law has reached. This law seems to increase and change every day. It spreads its tentacles throughout the internet and our only advice, when declaring our intention not to describe what it is, is to suggest that honesty in business is always the best policy and, if you always aim for that principle when selling, especially on the internet, you should be in the clear.

Data protection

It is very rare for a business not to have to register under the Data Protection Act. While all business users will be aware of the need to keep their records about others securely, many also find it perplexing trying to work out how by registering with the Information Commissioner's Office (ICO), their records will be any more secure than if they don't. Nonetheless, it is a legal requirement in most cases for businesses to register with the ICO and they can do so via the website www.ico.gov.uk.

The confidentiality issue of data protection is clearly important and in chapter 8 we provide some tips on how best to secure your data.

It is not considered the business of this book to start a discussion on how or when a businessperson is at liberty to disclose confidential information but the above website has plenty of information about this, should you be interested.

Employment law including tax law on paying wages

This is dealt with under chapter 4 of this book.

Equal opportunities

Employers are now forbidden to discriminate against people who are either seeking work with them or who are already working for them, or who are customers or potential customers of the firm, on the basis of any of the individuals' race, gender, disability, sexuality, age, religion or belief.

While we are experienced accountants, we are not trained lawyers and can only give the broadest of introductions to the topic of business law. However, in our experience, the best way of dealing with this matter appears to be that of ensuring that wording similar to the previous paragraph is included in the standard employment contract (see chapter 4).

Estoppel

This is one of those terms that you see bandied about but about which you tend to be too shy to show your ignorance by asking what it means. What it means is that, if you say, or assert, something (say in an advertisement) and someone acts on your assertion, you cannot later say 'Oh, I never meant to say that'. The law of estoppel stops you wriggling out of your obligations.

Fraud

We assume that little need be said here. Fraud is a crime and there's not only a whole lot of laws that outlaw fraud but, don't forget, there is also the famous Fraud Squad; so don't go committing fraud!

Health and safety

The purpose of this legislation is to protect people against risks to health or safety arising out of work-related activities. As the Health and Safety Executive says:

'As an employer you have a legal responsibility to protect the health and safety of your staff and other people – such as customers and members of the public – who may be affected by their work.

In general, employers must:

- make the workplace safe and eliminate or control risks to health;
- ensure plant and machinery are safe and that safe systems of work are set and followed;
- ensure articles and substances are moved, stored and used safely;
- provide adequate welfare facilities;
- give workers the information, instruction, training and supervision necessary for their health and safety;
- Consult workers on health and safety matters.'

While mentioning health and safety it would be no bad thing to cover the matter of fire regulations and businesses. Clearly, again, this is an area where professional advice should be sought, from the local fire authority; however, we include some key fire risk questions in chapter 8 TTC 3.04. Health and safety is covered in more depth in Lawpack's *Health & Safety at Work Essentials* book.

Intellectual property law

Intellectual property (IP) law is the area of law that deals with the protection of intellectual property, patents, copyrights, trademarks and trade secrets.

It overlaps with several other areas of law, such as patent law, copyright law and trademark law.

IP is an intangible form of property which tends to be the result of the creation of the brain or the mind. Examples include images, symbols, names, designs, industrial processes and business methods used in commerce; trade secrets; inventions; artistic, literary and musical works; and software. To protect any of these one should take proper legal advice.

Trademarks, patents and copyrights represent the ownership of an original idea for a limited period of time.

Artistic and creative works such as paintings, music, books, photographs, movies and software may be protected by copyright law.

International trade law

Again we can give no full, nor up-to-date, summary of what this huge subject covers. It is quite beyond the scope of this book and appropriate professional advice must be sought.

Non-disclosure agreement

This is an important aspect of business law that businesspeople, who have chosen to ignore it, have lived to rue the day. What it is about is (say) you have invented a gizmo and you take it to a manufacturer to ask him to produce and sell it for you; if you don't get that manufacturer to sign a non-disclosure agreement AT YOUR FIRST MEETING, in law he might well be free to say to himself, 'That gizmo looks like a truly wonderful business opportunity. The inventor has not got us to sign a non-disclosure agreement. Let's copy what he's done, manufacture and sell it ourselves and keep him out of the loop. No money for him – all of it for us.' That scenario has happened all too often.

Partnership law

When a business is run as a partnership, the partners need to be aware of one vital aspect – that of 'joint and several liability'. What this liability means is that, in the case of a partnership of (say) four partners, if that business goes bust and three of the partners are unable to pay its debts, the fourth partner will be responsible for ALL of the debts, not for just one quarter of them. This is why it can be dangerous for a husband and wife to go into partnership together. If that business were to go bust, the family home would be in the firing line. It is usually better for spouses not to join each other in partnership for this very reason.

It is not essential for a formal partnership deed to be drawn up but, if ever there are any doubts that a business partnership exists, it can be very helpful to produce the deed as evidence. Such a deed can also prove vital if one of the partners were to die and a row develops between the parties involved as to what is to happen to the partnership assets. The partnership deed would give the parties clear instructions on what should happen following the death of a partner.

Before a partnership deed is prepared it can be helpful to the solicitor to be given a document called 'the heads of agreement' by the proposed partners. This lists, in informal terms, how the partners want the partnership to be set up, and we provide a suggested sample heads of agreement in chapter 8 TTC 1.03.

Product liability

Businesspeople must be aware that, having supplied the product, they are liable for any injury that may be caused by the use, or malfunction, etc. of that product.

This area of the law is covered by consumer protection law and, as you can imagine, this law gives extensive protection to customers.

This liability is often covered by product liability insurance. Please see chapter 6 on insurance.

Property law

This area of the law governs, as you would expect, property. In this case property means 'real property' as opposed to intellectual property.

Businesspeople need to be aware of their responsibilities under this law in connection with:

- Occupation of business premises
- What are their obligations to:

  a) the local authority;

  a) the local community;

  a) any landlord;

  a) any visitor to their premises;

  a) any occupier of their premises, etc.?

- The right to occupy the property
- The rights to transfer property
  Etc.

When in doubt, seek professional legal advice.

Sale of Goods Act

As you have already seen, if you sell goods or services, you have certain responsibilities. What you sell must be as you describe them. This is known as 'conforming to contract'. Product and service descriptions must be accurate, whether written or verbal, and if what you sell does not conform to contract then you could be sued for breach of contract. The goods must also be safe, work properly and have no defects.

This law covers the rights of a customer to complain and how businesses are under a duty to deal with complaints properly and offer refunds where appropriate.

What the law does not say, but prudent businesses tackle with a positive and not a negative approach, is that, rather than treating complaints as a real body blow, businesses should welcome them as opportunities for a) learning a lot about how customers see their products – so the trader can improve them where necessary – but also b) if a complaint is handled properly, with the customer given not only fulsome apologies but also generous refunds and recompenses, that customer, rather than moaning about the business and product involved, will actually become an advocate for that business when he says how wonderfully his complaint was dealt with and how fulsomely he recommends others to take advantage of the magnificent customer service he received.

Tax law

This, like company law, is a huge subject and we recommend that you refer to our sister publication *Tax Answers at a Glance* available from www.lawpack.co.uk.

The law of tort

It always surprises us that the word tort is not used more often. We keep hearing of crimes and criminals, when people break the law of the land, but very seldom of torts, or tortfeasors (those who commit a tort) .

A criminal is someone who breaks the law of the land. A tortfeasor is someone who breaches a civil duty owed to someone else. When you hear of someone being awarded damages, they are usually paid by the tortfeasor. It may not surprise you to learn that the most prominent tort liability is negligence.

CHAPTER 4

Employment law

The multifarious ways in which the laws of the land affect employment are so convoluting as to make it almost impracticable to attempt to summarise them in just one chapter of a book on business management.

From the Sex Discrimination Act, through the rules governing unfair dismissal to the Equality Act, including the Working Time Directive, and not forgetting the workings of tax law and the rules governing the minimum wage, disability, and maternity pay (in fact the list appears to be endless), one has to readily admit that it is all a minefield.

Nonetheless, with so many employers taking people on, it is essential that we try to achieve the impossible and give employers a proper taste of what they are up against when they start to take people on. As we say it will be impossible to give anything more than an overview but, with so few employers bothering with even the elements of employment law (probably because they have no idea just how extensive their responsibilities really are), it is essential that we at least try to cover the basics of the basics.

Employment contracts

Let's start with the item that few employers actually start with, namely issuing employees with a proper contract of employment. It is quite extraordinary that with so many of us having a job – the thing that determines how we spend our weekday daylight hours – so few of us are actually issued with a proper contract determining the rules that govern that activity.

Our aim in this book is to give some easy-to-adopt assistance to people in business and so what we have done include the standard Lawpack employment agreement template – see chapter 8 TTC 4.10 – and then a short list of the topics one might find in a staff handbook - see chapter 8 TTC 4.11.

As you can see, you don't *have* to have a contract that's been drawn up by a lawyer (although lawyers would tend to disagree with that remark) and so, if you draw up a set of employment terms that are a) sensible, b) fair and, above all, c) agreed by your employees, and in line with the standard Lawpack template, that should be enough.

That said, problems can crop up at, for example, employment tribunals or, sometimes, with Her Majesty's Revenue & Customs (HMRC), and we make no pretence that our suggested form of contract will see you safe in every eventuality (one doubts whether there could ever be such an effective contract), but if the authorities can see that you have tried your best to provide your employees with a suitable contract, what we suggest in this book will go a long way towards keeping them happy. A growing number of employees use the services of a human resources (HR) consultant; they are not cheap, but if you follow their advice you are more than likely to avoid trouble than if you don't.

PAYE

Let's then move on to operating PAYE (Pay [tax] As You Earn). This is the bit that most employers usually farm out to payroll bureaux. It would not be possible to go into how PAYE works – that is covered in more depth in our sister publication *Tax Answers at a Glance* – but employers must ensure that they deal with aspects of Income Tax and NI deduction properly.

The first thing they must do is register with HMRC that they have taken someone on. You can do this online.

They must then apply the rules of deducting tax and National Insurance properly. If the employer is not using a payroll bureau, then we strongly advise them to buy a payroll program, or use the facility on the HMRC website.

Employers should be given a tax code by the new employee and, armed with a computerised program of sorts, it should all be plain sailing.

Can the employee be treated as 'self-employed'? Please refer to TTC 4.02.

Interviewing for new employees

Advertising and interviewing new employees is a time-consuming and sometimes tortuous job. There are a number of legal hoops you will have to go through and our aim in this book is to give you as many templates as we can to help.

These are:

1. Phrasing a job advert for the local paper or for placing on your website

2. Answering a job applicant who will not be called for interview – chapter 8 TTC 4.04

3. Answering a job applicant who will be called for interview – chapter 8 TTC 4.05

4. A suggested CV layout for the applicant to complete – chapter 8 TTC 4.01

5. A suggested template for the interviewer to complete before, during and after the interview – chapter 8 TTC 4.06.

6. A suggested letter refusing the interviewee the job – chapter 8 TTC 4.09

7. A suggested letter making a job offer – chapter 8 TTC 4.07

8. A suggested letter asking for an employee reference – chapter 8 TTC 4.12.

Things to do when making a job offer

When making a job offer it is usually wise to include the following conditions, namely that the offer is subject to:

- a trial period;
- satisfactory references being received;
- medical checks;
- checks on essential qualifications;
- the right to work in the UK;
- satisfactory criminal record checks;
- proper personal identification having been established.

Until the conditions have been fulfilled there is no contract between the two parties and the offer can be withdrawn by the employer.

Checking on the right to work in the UK

Employers must check the right of every successful candidate to work in the UK and this is done by asking the proposed employee to produce one of these forms of identification:

- Passport
- National identity card
- UK birth certificate
- And a whole range of others, the extent of which can be found by consulting the Department for Work and Pensions.

With certain employees (those who have only been granted permission to stay in the UK for a limited amount of time) you will have to check these documents again when they are renewed.

When looking at these documents you should check, as best you can, that the details are correct and consistent with what you would expect. You should check that the dates have not expired.

You should then make photocopies of what you have been presented with and keep the copies.

There can be severe penalties for failing to do this properly. These could be up to £10,000 for each illegal worker.

Trial periods

Trial periods (or probationary periods) of employment are an ideal method for both the employee and the employer to establish the job is right for him and he is right for the job.

While this is seldom mentioned, it is a good idea, if someone is being asked to leave because he has not come up to scratch during his trial period, for him to be paid an extra month – so that if the trial period was for three months, he would be paid for four months – to give him some help while he looked for another job. He should not be required to work for that extra month.

Statutory pay, maternity pay and paternity pay

The rules for paying this are fairly simple and reference should be made to the PAYE leaflets that you, as an employer, will have been given.

Sickness absence

Employees are entitled to Statutory Sick Pay and many employers offer some enhancement to this but there is no legal requirement to do so.

Training and time off for training

The rules for this only apply to employers with more than 250 employees. For such employers the rules are as follows:

Employees must work for at least six months before they can make a request to be given time off for training, although employees under the age of 18 can make a request at any time in their employment. The training does not necessarily have to lead to a qualification.

The employee should put the application in writing and it can be refused if the employer believes that the training would not improve the employee's effectiveness.

Retirement age

The default retirement age of 65 was abolished with effect from 6 April 2011. This means that employers can no longer require their employees to retire at the age of 65. An employee's 65th birthday marks the State Retirement Age (SRA).

An employer is entitled to withdraw some employment benefits, such as private medical insurance from employees when they reach SRA. An employee is now entitled to retire at an age that suits him.

Holidays

There is a minimum right to paid holiday, but an employer may offer more than this. The main things you should know about holiday rights are that:

- An employee is entitled to a minimum of 5.6 weeks' paid annual leave – 28 days for someone working five days a week (capped at a statutory maximum of 28 days for all working patterns).

- Part-time workers are entitled to the same level of holiday pro rata (so 5.6 times their usual working week, e.g. 22.4 days for someone working four days a week).

- An employee starts building up holiday as soon as he starts work.

- An employer can control when an employee takes his holiday.

- Employees get paid their normal pay for their holiday.

- When an employee finishes a job, he gets paid for any holiday he has not taken.

- Bank and Public Holidays can be included in an employee's minimum holiday entitlement.

- An employee continues to be entitled to holiday leave throughout her or his ordinary and additional maternity leave and paternity and adoption leave.

In order to qualify for the right to annual leave an employee needs to be classed as a worker. The self-employed have no statutory right to paid annual leave.

An employer may give more than the minimum 5.6 weeks' leave as part of their terms of employment.

An employee has no right to additional holiday, even if it's unpaid, unless his contract provides for it. Employers can set their own rules on any holidays they give over and above the legal minimum. An employer is not allowed to give an employee less than the legal minimum.

Public and Bank Holidays

Employees do not have a statutory right to paid leave on Bank and Public Holidays. If an employer gives paid leave on a Bank or Public Holiday, this can count towards an employee's minimum holiday entitlement. There are eight permanent Bank and Public Holidays in England and Wales (nine in Scotland and ten in Northern Ireland).

If an employee works on a Bank or Public Holiday, there is no automatic right to an enhanced pay rate. What an employee gets paid depends on your contract of employment.

If an employee is part time and the employer gives workers additional time off on Bank Holidays, this should be given pro rata to the part-time staff as well, even if the Bank Holiday does not fall on your usual work day.

Discipline

Employers need to deal with issues of discipline promptly.

When informal discussions cannot bring about a solution then the employee should be invited to a meeting to give his views. If there is no satisfactory explanation, the employee should be given the first written warning.

If that does not resolve the situation, a second meeting should be convened and if that does not resolve the problem, the employee should be given a final written warning.

If that does not work, then the employee may be dismissed or transferred or demoted.

In the case of any such meeting it is highly desirable for both parties to be accompanied by another so that, in the event of a claim for unfair dismissal, satisfactory evidence can be produced to show whether proper procedures for dealing with the situation were followed.

Grievances

If an employee has a grievance, he should notify the employer, following which a meeting should be held at which the employee should attend with someone to accompany him.

Following that meeting it should be decided what action to take.

If the employee is not satisfied, he should be allowed to take the grievance further by appealing, at which the procedure is repeated until a satisfactory outcome is reached.

If, during a disciplinary case, a grievance is raised, then the disciplinary case may be suspended until the grievance issues have been resolved.

Equal pay

An employer could find that their business is subject to an equal pay audit, the aim of which is to ensure that women are not being paid less than men for doing the same work.

Agency workers

With effect from 1 October 2011, an agency worker after 12 weeks with the same employer is entitled to the same terms and conditions of work as someone else in that firm doing the same job.

Discrimination

This is now covered by the Equality Act 2010. What this law now means is that you are not allowed to discriminate against either your employees (be they full time, part time, apprentices, self-employed or sub-contract, etc.) or your interviewees on the grounds of:

- Age
- Disability
- Gender reassignment
- Marriage and civil partnership
- Pregnancy and maternity
- Race
- Religion or belief
- Sex
- Sexual orientation.

The above are called protected characteristics.

So what is discrimination?

Discrimination is actually an odd word to use. In the 'old days' if you described someone as 'discriminating', you would imply that he was a thoughtful, careful person who made strong distinction between what he thought was right or wrong – in short a discriminating person was a praiseworthy person. Now that has all changed and discrimination is against the law.

You are guilty of discrimination if you treat someone less favourably:

- because of a protected characteristic; or

- because he associates with someone who has a protected characteristic; or

- because others think he possesses a protected characteristic; or

- if you have a policy or rule that applies to everyone except those who have a protected characteristic.

When might you fall foul of this law?

- In your job descriptions

- When assessing candidates.

What else does the Act cover?

Harassment

Employees can now complain if they are on the receiving end of harassment which can include:

- if they spot discriminating behaviour, even if it is not directed at themselves; or

- if a third party spots discriminating behaviour (a customer perhaps).

Victimisation

Victimisation occurs when an employee has raised a grievance under this Act and is treated badly as a result.

Dismissal and length of notice

Dismissal

An employee can bring a claim for unfair dismissal on the following grounds:

- Discrimination on grounds of sex, race, disability, or sexual orientation

- Pregnancy

- For seeking to exercise a statutory right

- Where an employee refuses to work in a situation which the employee believes to be contrary to his good health

- Whistle blowing

- Reasons relating to Jury Service.

The fair reasons for dismissal are:

- Sickness

- Poor performance

- Persistent lateness

- Theft

- Gross misconduct

- Redundancy

- Lack of ability or skill

- Long-term sickness.

Length of notice

The minimum period of notice depends on length of service:

Service	Notice entitlement
Less than one month	Nil
One month to two years	1 week
Two years	2 weeks
Three years	3 weeks
... *and so on up to*	
Twelve years	12 weeks

Redundancy

First of all what is redundancy?

This is the definition for tax purposes:

'An employee who is dismissed shall be taken to be dismissed by reason of redundancy if the dismissal is attributable wholly or mainly to:

- the fact that his employer has ceased, or intends to cease, to carry on the business for the purposes of which the employee was employed by them, or has ceased, or intends to cease, to carry on that business in the place where the employee was employed or

- the fact that the requirements of that business for employees to carry out work of a particular kind, or for employees to carry out work of a particular kind in the place where he was so employed, have ceased or diminished or are expected to cease or diminish.'

So how does redundancy pay work?

An employee that is made redundant may be entitled to statutory redundancy pay if he has worked for the same employer for at least two years. The amount he is entitled to will be based on his weekly pay, age and continuous employment with that employer.

Statutory redundancy pay is also due when a fixed-term contract of two years or more expires and is not renewed because of redundancy.

An employer is expected to pay an employee automatically. If this does not happen, the employee can appeal to an employment tribunal.

How much statutory redundancy pay an employee will receive depends on:

- how long the person has worked for your employer;
- his age;
- his pay.

Company redundancy pay

An employer may offer additional redundancy pay under the employment contract. For example, they may offer a higher pay rate, or reduce the qualifying criteria so more people are entitled. You should check the employment contract for details about the contractual redundancy pay.

An employer cannot offer lower than the statutory redundancy pay scheme in an employment contract.

Offering alternative work

An employee is not entitled to a statutory redundancy payment if the employer either:

- offers to keep the employee on; or
- offers suitable alternative work which the employee refuses without good reason.

If an employees leaves his job for a new one before the end of the notice period, his statutory payment might also be affected.

Short-term and temporary lay-off of employees

Statutory redundancy pay can be claimed from an employer if an employee has been temporarily laid off for either:

- more than four weeks in a row;

- more than six non-consecutive weeks in a thirteen-week period.

An employee should write to his employer telling them he intends to claim statutory redundancy pay. This must be done within four weeks of his last non-working day in the four- or six-week period.

Within seven days of receiving that letter, the employer could send a counter-notice if they believe that the employee's normal work is likely to start within four weeks and continue for at least thirteen weeks. If an employer does not reject such a claim within seven days of receiving it, then the employee should write to his employer again giving them his notice.

Notice pay

As well as a statutory redundancy payment, an employer should pay an employee through the notice period, or pay him in lieu of notice depending on circumstances. Payment in lieu of notice (PILON) is money paid by an employer as an alternative to an employee being given full notice. Details of the notice period will be in your employment contract.

Written statement of statutory redundancy pay

When an employee is paid a statutory redundancy payment the employer must give a written statement showing how his payment has been calculated. If the employer fails to give a written statement, the employee should write to ask for one. If the employer still does not provide one, the employee should seek further advice from ACAS (the Advisory, Conciliation and Arbitration Service).

Insolvent employers

In case this is not already clear, redundancy pay is payable by the employer, not the government. However, if an employer is declared insolvent or cannot pay statutory redundancy pay, an employee can apply for a direct payment from the National Insurance Fund. To do this he must first write to his employer asking for statutory redundancy pay. If they are still unable to pay, the employee should fill out an RP1 form available from the Insolvency Service.

Employees not entitled to statutory redundancy payments

Some employees are not entitled to receive statutory redundancy payments. In some specific situations employees that should normally be entitled to statutory redundancy pay might lose this right with their employer.

Finding a new job

If an employee has been selected for redundancy, he may find a new job elsewhere before the redundancy notice period has finished. If he leaves the job from which he is being made redundant from before his notice period has finished, he may lose his rights to a statutory redundancy payment.

Dismissal on the grounds of misconduct

Employees are not entitled to statutory redundancy pay if they are dismissed for misconduct with either:

- no notice;
- little notice; or
- a statement from an employer saying the employer would have been entitled to dismiss the employee without notice.

However, the employer must still follow fair dismissal procedures otherwise the employee might be able to make a claim to an employment tribunal. This situation is only likely to occur in gross misconduct cases.

Employees not entitled to redundancy payment

If an employee falls into one of the following categories then he is not entitled to receive statutory redundancy pay:

- Members of the armed forces
- House of Lords and House of Commons staff
- Some apprentices – although you should check your contract
- Some employees with fixed-term contracts before 1 October 2002 – you should check your contract of employment

- Domestic servants working in private homes who are members of the employer's immediate close family

- Share fishermen paid only by a share in the proceeds of the catch

- Crown servants or employees in a public office

- Employees of the government of an overseas territory.

Employees should check their contract or speak to their employer to see if they have any contractual redundancy entitlements.

How much redundancy pay is due?

How much redundancy pay is payable depends on the wage, length of service and age. You can find out how it is calculated by using the online calculator at www.gov.uk. Or you can calculate it as follows:

An employee will get:

- 0.5 week's pay for each full year of service where his age was under 22

- 1 week's pay for each full year of service where his age was 22 or above, but under 41

- 1.5 week's pay for each full year of service where his age was 41 or above.

For example, if he is 45, his weekly pay is £400 per week and he had completed 15 years' full service, he will receive £6,800 statutory redundancy pay.

Step 1: 1.5 weeks x 4 years' full service aged 41 or above = 6 weeks

Step 2: 1 week x 11 years' service when he was under 41 = 11 weeks

Step 3: 6 weeks + 11 weeks = 17 weeks x £400 = £6,800

Tax

Redundancy pay under £30,000 is not taxable. More information on whether elements of the payment, such as pay in lieu of notice (PILON), is taxable is available from HMRC. Pay in lieu of notice is money paid to an employee by an employer as an alternative to being given his full notice.

Employment tribunals

These tribunals are used for assessing whether someone has been unfairly dismissed and will look at three things:

1. Was the complainant dismissed?

2. Was the dismissal justifiable in the circumstances?

3. Was the way in which the dismissal was made, reasonable?

If the tribunal finds that the person was unfairly dismissed, the remedies available are:

- reinstatement of the person to the workforce under the same terms; or

- re-engagement with the same employee but for a different job.

Financial compensation for the loss of employment: there is a maximum award of £12,000 and it is calculated in the same way as redundancy pay. However, there is also a maximum compensatory award of £68,400 to compensate for actual loss of earnings, benefits and future losses although if the reason for dismissal was discrimination there is no cap.

There is also additional compensation payable when an employer refuses to reinstate an employee. Again this is at £400 per week with a maximum payable of £20,800.

National Minimum Wage (NMW)

This is increased every October and the current rates can be found at www.gov.uk.

There is one area in particular that should be stressed about this, namely that HMRC sends inspectors to see if employers are indeed paying according to the NMW rates.

Pensions and pension reform

There will be more pensioners in the future and most of those pensioners will live longer. This will put a massive strain on the State pension system.

To alleviate this burden, the Pensions Acts 2007 and 2008 make changes to the Basic State Pension, the State Second Pension and introduce new employer duties for pensions.

The employer duties

From October 2012, employers are required by law to:

- automatically enrol all their eligible employees not already in a good-quality pension scheme into a Qualifying Workplace Pension Scheme (QWPS) on the day the employee becomes eligible; and

- pay contributions for every employee who does not opt out of the QWPS.

Timetable

Employer duties are staged in over four years from 2012. Larger employers have their duties imposed first, smaller employers last. Any employer with fewer than 50 employees have their staging date set depending on the last two digits of their PAYE reference number.

Size of employer	Staging date
120,000 – 800	Over 12 dates from 1 October 2012 to 1 October 2013
799 – 250	Over 3 dates from 1 November 2013 to 1 February 2014
Fewer than 50 (sample)	On 1 March 2014
249 – 50	Over 4 dates from 1April 2014 to 1 July 2014
Fewer than 50	Over 18 dates from 1 August 2014 to 1 February 2016
New businesses that start up after October 2012	Over 5 dates from 1 March 2016 to 1 September 2016

Costs

The amount of contributions that must be paid in order for a scheme to be treated as a QWPS is being phased in as follows:

Date	Total minimum contribution %	Minimum employer contribution %	Minimum difference to be made up by employee % (gross)*
October 2012 to September 2016	2%	1%	1%
October 2016 to September 2017	5%	2%	3%
October 2017 onwards	8%	3%	5%

The contributions will be based on a percentage of band earnings between £5,035 and £33,540 (qualifying earnings) at 2006/7 levels. These amounts will be increased in line with earnings to 2012 and beyond.

* The minimum difference includes tax relief available on employee contributions.

Quality Qualifying Workplace Pension Scheme (QQWPS)

Employers can avoid much of the administration burden associated with automatic enrolment by setting up a QQWPS where:

- the total minimum contribution is 11 per cent of qualifying earnings, of which:

    a) at least 6 per cent must come from the employer;

    b) there is no option to phase in contributions; and

    c) automatic enrolment dates can be postponed up to 90 days allowing a 'sweep-up' of eligible employees all at once at the employer's convenience.

Eligible employees

All employees will have to be auto-enrolled unless:

- they are already in a Qualifying Workplace Pension Scheme;
- they are under the age of 22;
- they are over the State Pension Age; or
- they earn less than £5,035 a year (in 2006/7 terms).

Employees can only 'opt-out' once they have been auto-enrolled.

Non-eligible employees must be given the option of opting in to pension saving.

Auto-enrolment is the responsibility of the employer, not the government or the pensions industry. The Pensions Regulator will oversee employer compliance and has the power to fine employers for non-compliance.

National Employment Savings Trust (NEST)

Employers who do not have, or who will not set up, their own QWPS will have the option of using NEST. This scheme is designed to be low cost and is specifically aimed at low to medium earners. Restrictions applying to NEST will be:

- a general ban on transfers in or out;
- an upper contribution limit (currently £3,600 each year);
- limited retirement options; and
- limited investment options.

Effect on your business

These changes represent a substantial opportunity to set up QWPSs or QQWPSs ahead of 2012 to minimise the impact of the employer duties on your corporate clients. The risks are that:

- employers with existing schemes will level down contributions to the legislative minimum; and

- individual clients paying regular contributions may stop after 2012 when they are auto-enrolled into their employer's pension scheme.

Working Time Directive

No employee has to work for more than 48 hours a week on average, unless he chooses to, or work in a sector with its own rules. The normal working hours should be set out in the employment contract or written statement of employment particulars.

The weekly maximum working hours

Adult workers cannot be forced to work more than 48 hours a week on average – this is normally averaged over 17 weeks. They can work more than 48 hours in one week, as long as the average over 17 weeks is less than 48 hours per week.

An employee's working week is not covered by the working time limits if he has a job:

- where he can choose freely how long he will work (e.g. a managing executive);

- in the armed forces, emergency services and police – in some circumstances;

- as a domestic servant in private houses;

- as a sea transport worker, a mobile worker in inland waterways or a lake transport worker on board seagoing fishing vessels.

Since 1 August 2009 the 48-hour maximum working hours apply to trainee doctors.

Opting out of the 48-hour week

An employee aged 18 or over who wishes to work more than 48 hours a week, can choose to opt out of the 48-hour limit. This must be voluntary and in writing. It can't be an agreement with the whole workforce.

An employee may not be sacked or unfairly treated (e.g. refused promotion or overtime) for refusing to sign an opt-out.

An employee can cancel his opt-out agreement whenever he wants – even if it is part of his employment contract. However, he must give his employer at least seven days' notice. This could be longer (up to three months) if he had previously agreed this in writing with his employer.

An employer is not allowed to force an employee to cancel his opt-out agreement.

Example of opt-out agreement

I [*name*] agree that I may work for more than an average of 48 hours a week. If I change my mind, I will give my employer [*amount of time – up to three months*] notice in writing to end this agreement.

Signed: _____

Dated: _____

What counts as work?

As well as carrying out his normal duties, an employee's working week includes:

- job-related training;

- job-related travelling time, for example if he is a sales rep;

- working lunches, for example business lunches;

- time spent working abroad, if he works for a UK-based company;

- paid and some unpaid overtime;

- time spent on-call at the workplace.

What does not count as work?

Your working week does not include:

- breaks when no work is done, such as lunch breaks;

- normal travel to and from work;

- time when you are on call away from the workplace;

- evening and day-release classes not related to work;

- travelling outside of normal working hours;

- unpaid overtime that you have volunteered for, so for example staying late to finish something off;

- paid or unpaid holiday.

Young workers

A young worker is someone under 18 but over school leaving age. Young workers may not normally work more than eight hours a day or forty hours a week. The hours can't be averaged out for young workers.

There is no opt-out for young workers.

Working two different jobs

If an employee works for more than one employer, the amount of combined hours he works shouldn't exceed the 48-hour average limit.

If he works two jobs, he could either:

- consider signing an opt-out agreement with his employers if his total time worked is over 48 hours; or

- reduce his hours to meet the 48-hour limit.

Pay and work rights helpline

For confidential help and advice on working hours call 0800 917 2368.

Overtime

Overtime generally means any work over the basic working hours included in an employment contract. As we have just seen, Regulations say that most workers can't be made to work more than an average of 48 hours a week, but they can agree to work longer. This agreement must be in writing and signed by you.

Overtime pay

There's no legal right to pay for working extra hours, and there are no minimum statutory levels of overtime pay, although an employee's average pay rate must not fall below the National Minimum Wage. Your contract of employment should include details of overtime pay rates and how they are worked out.

Overtime rates vary from employer to employer; some will pay extra for working weekends or Bank Holidays, and others won't.

Time off instead of pay for working overtime

Instead of paying for overtime, some employers offer 'time off in lieu' (TOIL). This is agreed between an employee and his employer, and any time taken off will normally be at a time that suits the employer. Some companies have rules on when time off can be taken, but others arrange time off on a case-by-case basis.

Overtime and payment for time off

Overtime isn't usually taken into account when working out holiday pay or paid maternity, paternity or adoption leave. However, it is taken into account when the overtime is guaranteed and you have to work the overtime as part of your contract of employment.

Can an employee be forced to work overtime, or stopped from doing so?

The contract of employment should include the conditions for working overtime. An employee only has to work overtime if his contract says so. Even if it does, he can't usually be forced to work more than an average of 48 hours per week. If he is told to work more than this and he doesn't want to, he should take it up with his employer.

Overtime for part-time workers

Unless it says differently in their contract of employment, employers will usually only pay overtime to part-time workers when they work:

- longer hours than are included in their contract (although sometimes they might just get their normal rate);

- more than the normal working hours of full-time staff (when they must receive extra payments if full-time staff receive them);

- unsocial hours for which full-time staff would get more pay.

It is a legal requirement that part-time workers must not be treated less favourably than full-time staff.

Changes to patterns of work

An employer may need to change the conditions or patterns of work because of business or economic factors. However, the contract of employment can only be changed if both an employee and his employer agree to this. It's a breach of contract to change working conditions without an employee's agreement.

Work and families

There is a host of ever-changing rules about work and family life and we can only give you a brief overview of what they include.

You need to be aware of the following:

- **Pregnancy and maternity rights in the workplace**

    Working when pregnant

    Entitlements during Statutory Maternity Leave.

- **Paternity rights in the workplace**

    Ordinary Paternity Leave

    Additional Paternity Leave and Pay

    Entitlements during Ordinary Paternity Leave and returning to work.

- **Additional Paternity Leave**

    Fathers of babies born on or after 3 April 2011 could have the right to take up to 26 weeks' Additional Paternity Leave.

- **Adoption rights in the workplace**

    Statutory Adoption Leave (UK adoptions).

- **Parental leave and flexible working**

    Parental leave

    Taking parental leave

    Entitlements during parental leave and returning to work

    Flexible working

    Childcare

    Expecting or bringing up children (money, tax and benefits section).

For more information on the above you are advised to go to www.gov.uk.

CHAPTER 5
Business finance

This is a chapter on a subject where business authors have waxed lyrical over thousands and thousands of pages.

We are not going to say very much in this chapter, partly because so much has been said in these other works already; partly because most small businesspeople have little training, and even less inclination, to read pages and volumes on this subject and partly because we hope that the tips, templates and checklists we include provide the sort of essential practical advice that we hope you will find helpful.

But, while this chapter is being kept deliberately brief, it would do no harm to mention the six key things to remember when it comes to business finance. They are the following maxims:

1. Keep in close touch with your bank balance. Most people do this through online banking. It should be done daily whenever possible.

2. Prepare budgets and cash flow forecasts so you know what you hope will happen and are therefore better able to steer the business in the direction you want – see chapter 8 TTC 5.05 and 5.06.

3. Break down these forecasts into monthly periods.

4. Write up your transactions frequently; see chapter 8 TTC 5.11.

And then

5. Compare what actually happens with what you anticipated.

6. If things start to go wrong, tell your bank manager as soon as you see any problems ahead.

In addition, and in our view, if things start to go wrong, while it is tempting to cut costs as a reaction to your concerns, that is unlikely to make the business perform better. In other words, the business is more likely to make more money if you concentrate on growing sales rather than focussing solely on cutting costs.

And, if you want to grow your business, may we suggest you consider buying our book *101 Ways to Grow your Business*.

So what is the practical help we are going to try to give you under this heading?

The topics we think you will find helpful, and the relevant help we want to give you, are:

Topic	Chapter 8 TTC
How to understand accounts	5.09
The importance of Key Performance Indicators	5.03
How to approach a bank manager with a request for finance	5.01
What a full business plan looks like	5.02
How to hold a mini business planning session	5.04
What an accountant needs to prepare your accounts	5.10
The six steps to financial control	5.12

CHAPTER 6

Business insurance

With many thanks to Lorica Insurance Brokers for writing this chapter

General insurance is seen by many as an essential business expense that affects their bottom line profit. Due to this, many people will accept the cheapest offering without taking advice from an insurance professional. This can lead to gaps in policy coverage which, in turn, may lead to a claim being declined, negating the reason why insurance protection was purchased in the first instance.

There are many types of insurance product available to businesspeople including, but not limited to:

- **Property insurance and business asset protection**

    a) Buildings

    b) Stock and work in progress

    c) Machinery, plant and all other contents

    d) Computers, electronic business machines

    e) Business interruption

    f) Contract works and plant.

2. **General and legal liability**

    a) Public liability

    b) Products liability

    c) Employer's liability.

3. **Financial risks and management liability**

    a) Professional indemnity

    b) Directors' and officers' liability

    c) Employment practice liability

d) Environmental impairment liability.

We will now give the definition for insurance purposes for each of the above. The minimum level of cover you should consider is fire, theft, flood and storm. However, it is recommended that cover be placed on an all-risks basis, including accidental damage and subsidence. Suffice it to say that if you feel your current insurance arrangements are inadequate to provide full protection for your business, you should seek the advice of an insurance professional.

Buildings

The buildings and outbuildings situated at the premises including walls, gates, fences and landlord's fixtures and fittings in and on the premises, internal and external fixed glass, sanitary ware and signs, central heating systems and concrete, paved or asphalt forecourts, terraces, drives and footpaths.

Stock and work in progress

Stock and materials in trade, work in progress and finished goods owned by you or held by you in trust for which you are responsible.

Machinery, plant and all other contents

Machinery, plant fixtures and fittings and other trade equipment, all office equipment and other contents, money and stamps including National Insurance stamps, documents, manuscripts and business books, patterns, models, moulds and designs.

Computers, electronic business machines

Computers and electronic business machines for which you are responsible, including laser printers, fax machines and photocopiers.

Business interruption

Indemnity for loss of gross income/revenue/profit, beginning with the occurrence of the damage and ending not later than the number of months stated on the policy schedule during which the results of the business are affected as a result of the damage.

Contract works and plant

The permanent and temporary works executed in the performance of a contract and materials for use in connection with that, including own plant and tools and plant on hire.

Public liability

Indemnity against all sums that you become legally liable to pay as compensation, including costs and expenses in respect of accidental injury to any person, accidental loss of or damage to property, accidental nuisance or trespass, obstruction, and loss of amenities or interference with any right of way, light, air or water.

Products liability

Indemnity against all sums that you become legally liable to pay as compensation, including costs and expenses in respect of accidental injury to any person and accidental loss of or damage to property caused by any product supplied.

Employer's liability

Indemnity against all sums that you become legally liable to pay as compensation, including costs and expenses in respect of injury sustained by any employee caused within the territorial limits and arising out of the employment by you in the course of the business.

Professional indemnity

Indemnity in respect of third-party claims for financial loss alleged to have arisen from a negligent act, error or omission, during the provision of your professional services. Usually this concerns either legal or civil liability, with claims costs and expenses either inclusive or in addition to the limit of indemnity procured. Depending on the nature of the profession, policy coverage may also extend to include:

- Inadvertent breach of intellectual property rights
- Libel and slander
- Breach of confidentiality
- Loss of documents
- Dishonesty of employees.

Directors' and officers' liability

Indemnifies the directors and officers in respect of loss arising out of a claim for a wrongful act, error or omission which is alleged to have arisen while discharging their fiduciary responsibilities. Coverage may be restricted to the individuals, or may incorporate the entity itself, if corporate liability is included. Claims may arise from many areas, including breaches related to:

- Companies Act
- Health & Safety at Work Act
- Insolvency Act
- Data Protection Act.

Employment practice liability

Indemnifies the corporate entity in respect of claims costs and awards arising out of employment disputes. Coverage typically includes (but is not limited to) any actual or alleged:

- Discrimination
- Unfair, constructive or wrongful dismissal
- Sexual, racial or disability harassment
- Violation of an employee's civil rights.

Environmental impairment liability

Indemnifies the policyholder in respect of liability arising out of pollution of third-party land and property. Coverage can include not only claims costs and expenses, but also clean-up costs. In the UK, current legislation dictates that when a site becomes polluted, and the original polluter cannot be identified, the current landowner is responsible for cleaning up the site, regardless of whether they played any part in the original cause of the pollution.

Disclosure

It is your responsibility to provide complete and accurate information, including material facts, at the inception of cover. This responsibility continues throughout the lifetime of the policy or on the occasion of any substitution or amendment of cover or when a claim is made.

Material facts are those that would influence an insurer when deciding whether to accept the risk, and the terms and conditions that should apply. Failure to disclose any material fact or change of circumstances could invalidate your cover and lead to the declinature of a claim.

If you are not sure what constitutes a material fact, please discuss this with your insurance professional.

Unless you advise otherwise, please also note that on the occasion of any renewal of insurance that reliance will be made on the information previously provided by you in connection with the insurance policy or policies the subject of renewal.

Setting sums insured, policy estimates and indemnity values

The setting of and advising your insurers of the sums insured and/or indemnity values and/or policy estimates is always your responsibility, as insurers will rely on this information when deciding the policy terms and premiums to apply. If you are underinsured or have mis-stated policy estimates, insurers may refuse to pay a claim in full or in part.

CHAPTER 7
Selling a business

Planning your sale

Once you have bought a business, from as early as day one you really should be thinking about how you are going to sell it. Now, before we start to deal with the process and tax implications of selling a business, we do want to make an impassioned plea to all people wanting to get out of their business that they really should try to get some money for it. So often we see people walking away from a life's work with nothing in their pocket to show for it and the thought brings tears to our eyes.

As Michael Gerber, author of *The E-Myth*, says, 'If nobody buys your business, then the one person who has bought it is you'. Why spend a lifetime working in a business, building it up and making a living out of it and then merely closing it down when you want to retire? Why not take some money (hopefully good money) from which to live off during your retirement? So please make sure that you sell your business rather than shrug your shoulders, as so many do, and merely walk away.

But how should you set about selling it? What you have to do is turn your business into a product that someone will want to buy by giving it a wonderful wrapper so that it will attract attention. So how do you do this? Here are some issues you may want to address if you want to attract a buyer:

- The business premises look tired.
- Your profits have been stagnant.
- The overdraft had been steadily growing.

If you want to sell your business, you must think of the customer and make the product he is going to buy as attractively packaged as possible. On the other hand, if you simply decide one day that you would like to sell up and you ask your local business transfer agent to come and value it for you, the chances are that, if he turns up and sees the dirty carpet in reception, the tired coffee mugs, the scruffy way your people dress (because this is what any buyer will see), you will be heading for a disappointing price.

So if you want to sell your business (and as we have said before, you must think of how you will sell it a few years before you put it on the market), ask yourself as you look around your business today whether it looks attractive. Be honest. Would you want to buy it?

It might help you to get a trustworthy friend to come and walk around the business. Show him what you will be selling and ask him if he thinks you have packaged it sufficiently attractively for it to attract interest from a would-be buyer.

Now, bearing in mind that there is no such thing as a perfect business, there are bound to be things you could do to brush up the appearance of the business. You could:

1. Paint the outside of the premises.

2. Make sure that the windows look clean and are in a good state of repair.

3. Decorate the reception area so that as the potential buyers walk in they feel welcomed by the nice ambience, rather than put off by the dirt and the smell.

4. Prepare a nice brochure or folder. It needn't be an expensive one but it should be clearly laid out and contain all the information that a buyer will want to know. At the very least, this folder should contain:

    a) Why you want to sell

    b) Exactly what it is that you are selling

    c) Up-to-date accounts

    d) Latest management accounts

    e) Five years' worth of records of sales and profits

    f) Dividend history (if yours is a company that pays dividends)

    g) Recent valuations of assets that might be for sale

    h) A list of the dates that you acquired key items of equipment

    i) Details of products sold with gross profit percentages

    j) Examples of nice things that happy clients have said

    k) List of employees (you may not want to give their names but you should list the numbers of employees, who does what, their length of service and what they are paid)

    l) The names of the directors and how long they are expected to remain with the company (only applicable for companies)

    m) A family tree for your business.

n) List of current advisers:

  i) Bankers

  ii) Accountants

  iii) Solicitors

  iv) Printers

  v) Major suppliers

  vi) Major customers

  vii) Major competitors

  viii) Marketing advisers

o) Profit forecasts, in some detail

p) Your mission statement

q) A current action plan – what you are planning to do in the next few years

r) Latest customer newsletters.

The folder should have a contents sheet and clearly indexed tabs helping the would-be purchaser find what he is looking for. If possible, have your business name printed on the outside so that, even before he picks the folder up, he is beginning to feel impressed.

Lastly, you must make sure that your website is up to date and fresh. This will be the first place your would-be purchaser will look and if it appears that it hasn't been updated for a few months, it could well put off people from even bothering to ask to see the detailed folder.

Who is advising you over the sale?

When it comes to selling a business, which is something that you have built up into a significantly valuable asset, you should take advice and take it early on. You can use a business transfer agent, an accountant or a solicitor, but if you try to do it yourself, you are likely to get into a muddle and make less money than if you pay for good advice.

You may be tempted just to talk to your accountant or bank manager or possibly your solicitor and they should indeed be consulted about your plans, but if you want someone to hold your hand through the whole process of getting the best deal, presenting your business in the most attractive light and helping you with the negotiation, then we think you should hire a specialist valuer and business transfer agent (see chapter 2 for more information). A business transfer agent will help you to package your business so that it attracts the best possible price.

As an accountant, we've seen a business changing hands on the basis of what two friends have considered to be the best deal, and the sale went through without any legal documentation.

This lack of formality may return to haunt either of the parties. For one there may be a subsequent legal dispute and second, the taxman may challenge what has been agreed.

So pay for the best advice if you want to get the best and safest deal.

Valuing your business

Please forgive us if we repeat, more or less, what has already been said in chapter 2, but not only does it need repeating but also you will need to be very clear exactly what it is you are selling.

As before, we will not now try to tell you to value the business that you are contemplating selling. Not only is a valuation, like beauty, in the eye of the beholder but, with a matter as serious as this, you really do have to take professional advice. But you might like some general guidance.

The first rule of thumb, and it's only a general rule and the calculation depends on all sorts of other factors, is that a small business is worth three times its net profit. This is a good place to start.

If yours is a limited company and if the net profit has been calculated after deducting the proprietor's salary, then the sum for that salary should be added to the net profit before it's trebled to arrive at the valuation. This is because with you, the selling proprietor, no longer working in the business, this is a cost that the purchaser will no longer incur, and so the incoming proprietor can reasonably expect to be putting the profit plus the old proprietor's salary into his pocket or at his disposal.

However, if the incoming proprietor is unwilling to work in the business, then while the method of working out the valuation is unaffected by this, the new proprietor has to realise that his return will be the net profit, plus the old proprietor's salary less the salary he is going to pay to the manager he is going to appoint. This may affect the price he is prepared to pay, even though what he plans to do with the business after he has bought it will be no concern of yours.

There are other methods of valuation, of course, and these have been described in chapter 2. The Stock Exchange has all sorts of measurements but, for instance, if you are selling a professional firm, it's not uncommon for such businesses to be valued at one year's worth of recurring fees.

However, our personal favourite method is 'gut feeling'. If you have calculated the asking price, tarted up the look of the business, answered all the questions that may be asked of you, whether through a due diligence exercise or otherwise, and you feel that the price is right, then that surely is a better guide than any rough-and-ready formula that we might set out in this book?

If you refer back to 'How to value a business' in chapter 2, you will see that we have included a section on valuing your customer list. You may just want to sell your customers or part of them, should you wish to scale down your operations. However, do beware that, while the formula is generally an accepted one, in practice the prices reached for a customer list tend to be one year's purchase of net profits rather than the two years' that the textbooks say you should ask to be paid.

Finding a buyer

As we've already said, on the whole it's extremely rare for a buyer to knock on your door and ask you if you are prepared to sell your business. So don't bank on it happening. Expect to have to go looking for one or to hire a specialist to go looking for you.

In our opinion, and to repeat once more, the best people are business transfer agents. For a start, selling businesses is their job – it's what they are paid to do.

One of the key roles that they will play is to have a website of businesses for sale and once your business is up there, it will increase your chances of a successful sale. You are unlikely to attract the sort of attention you would like if you start the selling process yourself from scratch.

But, if you want to do it yourself, here are some ideas of how to attract interest:

- **Advertising:** If you put 'sell our business' into Google, you will find a number of business transfer agents and other websites where you can advertise what it is that you want to sell.

- **Approaching your competitors:** They may be interested in expansion and you may have got exactly what they want.

- **Approaching your suppliers and distributors:** Again, these people may want to expand. They already know you and your business may be just what they are looking for.

- **Individual investors:** Why not approach an individual who you know may be interested in buying your business? If you don't know where to find him, then why not write to the local solicitors and accountants who may know someone to introduce to you.

- **Corporate investors:** We would suggest that you approach such people through your existing professional advisers.

- **Flotation:** This means selling your shares on the Stock Exchange. It would only be for large businesses and, again, it would be through your professional advisers that an approach might be made.

- **Management buyouts (MBOs):** This is where you sell your business to one or more of your employees and for this you would need professional advice.

The tax implications on selling a business

As a practising accountant, we have to admit that it's not as easy to sum up the tax implications of the sale of a business as it is to sum up the tax implications of purchasing one. There are so many variables, such as:

- What are the tax written-down values of the assets that are for sale? These will not be the figures shown in your balance sheet.

- Are the assets you are selling included in the balance sheet at cost or a more recent valuation?

- How much has been written off through depreciation?

- What other circumstances and variables might you, personally, be bringing to the tax computations on the sale, such as:

  a) Entrepreneurs' Relief

     i) Will all the business attract Entrepreneurs' Relief?

     ii) How many years have you owned the assets?

  b) Your personal rate of tax

  c) Any other capital gains that you might have made during the relevant tax year.

The following example provides variables on calculating your tax, but please don't take what is written here as being the be-all and end-all of the matter so far as calculating what your personal tax bill will be at the end. You must take professional advice if you want an early estimate of how much the Chancellor is going to take when the sale is completed.

Example

We're going to assume that you are the proprietor of a small self-employed business because that seems to be the most common type of sale.

On the other hand, and just before we get to the tax implications of a self-employed person selling his business, if you own a limited company and you are selling the whole company, what you will get is cash for your shares. This sort of sale is really very straightforward. The calculation will be as follows:

	£	
Sale proceeds	100,000	
Less sum paid for the shares	(20,000)	
Chargeable gain qualifying for Entrepreneurs' Relief	80,000	
Less exemption	11,000	This is the 2014/15 figure
Gain chargeable to tax	69,000	
Capital Gains Tax payable (£69,000 x 10%)	6,900	

But let's now consider the reality of what might happen because when a business is sold, it's almost certain that each asset will have to be considered separately:

ASSET: FREEHOLD PROPERTY

How the gain on the sale will be taxed: If the freehold property is legally owned by a proprietor outside the business but shown in the balance sheet for business purposes, you will be looking at a Capital Gains Tax bill, assuming that you have made a gain.

In principle, you take the net sale proceeds (or the net proceeds attributable to the freehold property) and take off the costs of purchase, take off the costs of any improvements you have made, and look at the resulting gain.

You then take off the annual exemption (for 2014/15 this is £11,000) and apply the appropriate rate of Capital Gains Tax (either 18 per cent or 28 per cent, or a mixture of both, or if the property is eligible for Entrepreneurs' Relief, 10 per cent).

However, do beware that you are entitled to only one annual exemption each year. So if you have sold or even given away anything else in the same tax year, any gain on that disposal could well have already used up your annual exemption.

ASSET: LEASEHOLD PROPERTY

How the gain on the sale will be taxed: This can be very complicated but leases nowadays seldom seem to attract a premium so it may not present a tax problem. However, if you did pay a premium and are now receiving a premium as you sell, do be aware that there are complicated rules for taxing gains on lease premiums. Because leases are wasting assets, their cost for tax purposes diminishes over time and if you paid £5,000 for the lease and are now receiving £6,000, the gain you make for tax purposes will be more than £1,000.

ASSET: FIXTURES AND FITTINGS

How the gain on the sale will be taxed: You take the written-down value (which you get from your accountant) for tax purposes (which is very unlikely to be the same as the figure in the balance sheet) from the sale proceeds and you pay Income Tax on the difference.

ASSET: PLANT AND EQUIPMENT

How the gain on the sale will be taxed: You take the written-down value for tax purposes from the sale proceeds and you pay Income Tax on the difference.

ASSET: COMMERCIAL VEHICLES

How the gain on the sale will be taxed: You take the written-down value for tax purposes from the sale proceeds and you pay Income Tax on the difference.

ASSET: PRIVATE MOTOR VEHICLES

How the gain on the sale will be taxed: You take the written-down value for tax purposes from the sale proceeds. You thereby arrive at a figure of taxable profit or loss on the sale, but, because you are likely to have used this car for private purposes and this use will have reduced the tax allowance you have claimed (perhaps by a third each year), you then abate the profit or loss by this same percentage and pay Income Tax on the difference.

ASSET: INVESTMENTS

How the gain on the sale will be taxed: As with freehold property, investment assets are likely to attract Capital Gains Tax and not Income Tax. In principle, you take the net sale proceeds (or the net proceeds attributable to the sale of the investment), take off the costs of purchase, and look at the resulting gain. You then take off the annual exemption (for 2014/15 this is £11,000) and apply the appropriate rate of Capital Gains Tax (either 18 per cent or 28 per cent, or a mixture of both). However, do beware that you are entitled to only one annual exemption each year, so if you have sold or even given away anything else in the same tax year, any gain on that disposal could well have already used up your annual exemption.

ASSET: INTANGIBLE ASSETS WITH THE EXCEPTION OF THOSE BELOW

How the gain on the sale will be taxed: These are treated in the same way as investment sales.

ASSET: INTANGIBLE ASSETS IN THE FORM OF GOODWILL, PATENTS, TRADEMARKS, COPYRIGHT, KNOW-HOW, LICENCES, ETC.

How the gain on the sale will be taxed: Again, these are treated in the same way as investments but, in the case of goodwill, this only applies to companies. A sole trader cannot claim any writing-down allowance on goodwill.

ASSET: DEBTORS

How the proceeds of the sale will be taxed: It's common for vendors, particularly vendors of self-employed businesses, to collect their own debtors, so you may not be selling these in any event. However, whichever way you dispose of or realise your debtors, it's likely that the cash you receive will be treated through the profit and loss account.

It can be quite complicated trying to explain how debtors 'look after themselves' in this way, so far as tax is concerned, but if you think about it, you will see that any tax they attract will appear in your trading accounts and will form part of your Income Tax bill.

ASSET: STOCK AND/OR WORK IN PROGRESS

How the proceeds of the sale will be taxed: While negotiations about values for premises, plant and equipment, vehicles, etc. will normally have been based on the figures in the previous year's balance sheet, stock and work in progress are normally valued at the date of changeover and any cash you receive for them, as for debtors, will be included in sales proceeds for the final accounting period.

ASSET: LOANS

How the proceeds of the sale will be taxed: When these debts (loans) are repaid, on the assumption that you are repaid what you originally lent, you will not pay tax on that money.

> **ASSET: CASH BALANCES**
>
> **How the proceeds of the sale will be taxed:** It's usual for the vendor of a self-employed business to keep the cash that's in the bank at the date of sale and, as such, the receipt of that balance will not attract any tax liability.

How can you reduce the tax payable?

Again, this needs professional advice and saving tax does not necessarily mean that less money leaves your bank account, but here are a few ideas that may help in your case:

- Consider taking your spouse or other family member into the business or giving, or selling, him or her some shares. If you own a limited company, each of you will be entitled to an annual Capital Gains Tax exemption and this could reduce your tax bill very significantly.

- Think of paying family members who work in the business a handsome sum for compensation on losing their job. This needs careful handling but you might well find that there is a substantial tax saving for the family at large to be found in this area.

- The chances of paying yourself a handsome sum under the above facility are not that great but it might be worth investigating.

- If you pay any employees redundancy on the sale of your business, it would help your case for paying yourself and members of your family a larger tax-free sum if you pay your employees more than the statutory rates of redundancy.

- You may be able to make payments into a pension scheme.

- You may be able to roll over the gains on certain business assets by buying new business assets – Rollover Relief. However, do look carefully at the figures. It's not uncommon for it to make more sense to pay a small amount of Capital Gains Tax rather than pay none when the business is sold but have a larger tax debt always hanging over any future sale of the business into which you have rolled over the gain.

- If you decide to give business assets away, you may be able to elect to have the gain held over (Holdover Relief). This means that the person to whom you are giving the business assets takes them on at the cost you incurred and not at their value at the date of gift.

- If you have incurred trading losses from the business you are selling, you may be able to set them off against your capital gain on the sale of that business.

- If you leave the UK for tax residence abroad, you must be absent for at least five years if you wish the gain to be tax free.

One other point you should consider is, once the company has ceased all operations and has been sold, can you apply to Companies House to have the company struck off? The short answer is 'yes', but please beware of the rules called 'bona vocantia'. Unless you get it right, the government can legally step in and take great chunks of what is rightfully yours. Please take professional advice.

CHAPTER 8

Management tips, templates and checklists (TTCs)

Most management books are full of verbiage – and very good verbiage at that – but few, very few indeed, actually show you how to do management things. You will find lots of theory and calculations, graphs and diagrams, but very few actual guides as to how you should set about, for example, writing a letter or email to a job applicant inviting him to an interview, or how to write to him saying that he has got, or not got, the job.

This part of the *Small Business Handbook* is where we hope you will find that it scores where its rivals fail. This is where we hope you will get extra value for money from your purchase.

What we have done is arrange these management tips, templates and checklists into groups that correlate, roughly, with the chapters that have gone before; and then, at the end, we have added a host of other tips, templates and checklists that don't really fit under the headings already used, but which should be useful.

As we say at the start of this book, if there is anything here that you don't find helpful, or if there is a checklist that's missing and it's one you think we ought to include in a later edition, please let us know. If you send us a tip, template or checklist that we use, you will get a) a mention in the Acknowledgements page and b) a free copy of the next edition.

So what can you expect to find in this chapter?

CHAPTER	TTC	
1. Running a business	1.01	Checklist of things to do when starting a business
	1.02	Self-employment questionnaire – is it for me?
	1.03	Heads of agreement for a partnership agreement
	1.04	The importance of a mission statement
	1.05	The importance of a vision statement

CHAPTER	TTC	
2. Buying a business	2.01	Investors' aspiration form
	2.02	Possible sources of finance
3. Business law	3.01	Suggested terms of business
	3.02	Non-disclosure agreement
	3.03	Data protection recommendations
	3.04	Fire safety risk assessment
	3.05	Suggested shareholders' agreement
	3.06	Business names – what to do
	3.07	Notice of particulars of ownership
	3.08	Business stationery – what it must show
4. Employment	4.01	Suggested job application form
	4.02	Questionnaire to help you decide if an employee can be treated as self-employed
	4.03	Suggested plan for interviewing a new member of staff
	4.04	Letter not calling job applicant to interview
	4.05	Letter calling job applicant to interview
	4.06	Suggested format for interview notes
	4.07	Letter offering job
	4.08	New employee details
	4.09	Letter following failed interview
	4.10	Template contract of employment
	4.11	Suggested matters for staff handbook
	4.12	Letter asking for a reference
	4.13	Employee appraisal form
	4.14	Suggested holiday form
	4.15	Sample agreement when one spouse works for another
	4.16	What records does an employer have to keep?
	4.17	Sample job description
	4.18	Employee travel expense and/or mileage claim
	4.19	Plan for weekly management get together with individual member of staff
	4.20	Employee contact details suggested layout
	4.21	Additional suggested report of employee details
	4.22	Plan for quick weekly team briefing
	4.23	Other employee benefits that a business might provide
	4.24	Suggested self-employed contract form

CHAPTER	TTC	
4. Employment law (cont)	4.25	How to assess someone for possible redundancy
	4.26	How to calculate holiday entitlement
	4.27	Discrimination in the workplace
5. Business finance	5.01	How to approach a possible lender with a request for finance
	5.02	Sample full business plan
	5.03	KPIs
	5.04 .	Holding a mini business planning session
	5.05	Cash flow forecast sheet
	5.06	Budget sheet
	5.07	Income and expenditure account
	5.08	Layout of VAT invoice
	5.09	Understanding accounts
	5.10	What an accountant needs to prepare your accounts
	5.11	Sheet showing analysis of cash and cheques, etc. paid out
	5.12	The six steps to financial control
	5.13	What expenses can I claim against tax?
6. Business insurance	6.01	Suggested business continuity plan
	6.02	Schedule of equipment for insurance purposes
7. Selling a business	None	
8. Other tips, templates and checklists	8.01	The importance of delegation
	8.02	Make sure your debtors pay up
	8.03	How to set out a press release
	8.04	Sample agenda for a meeting
	8.05	Sample minutes of business meeting
	8.06	Tips on holding meetings
	8.07	The art of decision making
	8.08	Decision making – tackling difficult tasks
	8.09	Template for a customer survey
	8.10	Suggestions on writing a report
	8.11	Creating an organisation chart for your business
	8.12	New customer details
	8.13	Suggested telephone message sheet
	8.14	Suggested jobs to do list
	8.15	Tips on one-to-one training
	8.16	Creating a marketing plan

1.01 **Checklist of things to do when starting a business**

	See Tips, templates and checklists number	Tick when done ✔
Am I made of the right stuff – have I filled in the self-assessment questionnaire?	1.02	
Have I developed a vision of what I hope to achieve?	1.05	
Have I developed a mission statement?	1.04	
Do I have a rough budget for the first few years?	5.06	
Do I have a cash flow forecast plan for the first year?	5.05	
Do I know the main reasons for business failure?		
Have I decided whether to trade as self-employed or through a limited company or partnership?	Chapter 1	
Do I know the basic rules of running a business?	Chapter 1	
Have I opened a business bank account?	Chapter 1	
Do I have sufficient finance in place?		
Have I registered this business with HMRC?		
Have I registered with HMRC for VAT? Do I need to?		
Have I registered with HMRC as an employer? Do I need to?		
Do I know what to do about displaying a trading name?	3.06 and 3.07	
Have I appointed a chartered accountant?		
Do I need to tell my local authority that I am running a business?		
Do I need any special insurance cover?	Chapter 6	
Am I aware of the basics of business law?	Chapter 3	
Do I know how to keep my accounts?	Lawpack's *Self-Employment Kit*	
Have I made a marketing plan?	8.16	
Have I created a website for my business?		
Have I ordered business stationery, invoices and business cards?		
Do my customers know what my terms of business are?	3.01	

1.02 **Self-assessment questionnaire – is it for me?**

Are you made of the right stuff to run your own business? Use the following questionnaire to discover to what degree you possess these needed traits. Be honest with yourself when answering the questions. Nothing is gained by being untruthful; the only person you hurt is yourself.

Read each question or statement carefully. Reflect on how strongly you either agree or disagree with it. Show how you identify with each remark by scoring from 1 to 10 at the end of each statement. For example, 1 will indicate you disagree with the question. On the other hand, 10 will signify that you strongly agree, i.e. it sums up your character precisely.

In respect of the question 'Do I perform well under pressure?', if you concur that you do perform well when under pressure, enter 10. If you feel your work deteriorates under pressure, enter 1. If you believe working under pressure makes you feel uncomfortable, but your work doesn't suffer, enter 4, etc.

		Your score out of 10
1.	Do I perform well under pressure?	
2.	Do I stay calm and not get stressed?	
3.	Do I persevere when influences over which I have no control affect my life?	
4.	Can I work with, and lead, a team?	
5.	Am I prepared to make a plan for the future of my business and to revisit it regularly to see how things are turning out against this plan?	
6.	Does making decisions come easily?	
7.	Are the decisions I make usually the right ones?	
8.	Am I positive, and do I enjoy taking risks?	
9.	Am I prepared to delegate the work my business does to employees, so that I can concentrate on managing the business?	
10.	Do I work well using my own initiative?	
11.	Do I bounce back from setbacks and work at a problem until it's solved?	
12.	Does the thought of learning new skills and the responsibility of being my own boss excite me?	
13.	Do I have the ability to change my mind when it's obvious an earlier decision was wrong?	
14.	Does explaining things to others come easily, and am I patient if I am misunderstood?	
15.	How much might my spouse/partner object to my business interfering with our private lives? (no objection = 10)	
16.	Am I a good listener, and can I take advice from others?	
17.	Do I prefer to stand alone, rather than to be one of a crowd?	

Self-assessment questionnaire – is it for me? (continued)

18.	Do I enjoy meeting and dealing with different people?	
19.	Is having my success recognised by others important to me? (not important = 10)	
20.	Am I at present in good health, and rarely get sick?	
	Total:	

When you have answered all of the questions and statements, total your score. Look below to see how you shape up to becoming an entrepreneur. If in doubt, give your completed assessment questionnaire to a friend or relation you trust. Ask him for a fair appraisal of your abilities. Don't be afraid of criticism. Learning to accept your faults is another trait you'll need in your armoury. Learning to conquer your failings is the bedrock of successful businesses.

ASSESSMENT RESULTS

Look for the group into which your score falls. In addition, also reconsider any scores which were either extremely high or low; assess how accurate you have been.

180 to 200 If your score lies in this band, stress and pressure spur you on. You are dedicated and prepared to work hard to achieve your goals. The risk and insecurity of running your own business will motivate rather than worry you. You have every chance of success with the right business idea and sound planning.

140 to 179 Certain aspects of running your own business may give you problems. The severity of these will depend on your determination to overcome adversity. Concentrate on improving those areas where you did not have a high score. However, you seem to have the right frame of mind to deal with the day-to-day pressures of running a business. Your business should flourish and you'll probably enjoy the rewards more than those with a higher score.

100 to 139 If your scores varied wildly, such as a lot of 1, 2, 8 and 9s, you must try to improve the lower scores. Otherwise those regions could be the source of severe problems if you are unable to change them. If this score was reached with reasonably consistent scoring, you should have no cause for concern, but you must ensure that you have a good business plan and are prepared to make use of the various training schemes.

60 to 99 If your responses were born out of uncertainty, contact your local enterprise agency for details of training courses. While you may have the ability to run your own business, there are strong indications that you will not enjoy it. Not enjoying your business could cause you to give up under the slightest pressure. Think long and hard about whether you really want to run a business. If you still think going into business is for you, make use of the help and training that are readily available.

Under 60 Running your own business will be a strain – one you may not wish to endure for long. Running a business requires confidence, self-reliance and the competence to handle stress and pressure. Without these traits it would be unwise to set up your own business. You should find out about training courses in your local area to develop the skills you lack.

The above assessment results are only a general guide and only useful if you are frank and truthful. It is not an appraisal of your technical and commercial proficiency, but of your personal attributes, which could affect your business. It's basic and is only intended to give a broad idea of your aptitude. Visit www.gov.uk to search for business-related training in your area, since even with the right personality and attitude, some skills instruction may be beneficial.

1.03 **Heads of agreement for a partnership agreement**

'Heads of agreement' for a partnership agreement between two or more people, for example a husband and wife.

This is to certify that on _____ Mr and Mrs _____ agreed to enter into a _____ partnership to be based at _____.

The essential parts of their verbal agreement are:

1. Commencement date: _____.
2. Initial capital (jointly): _____.
3. There will be no entitlement of interest on capital.
4. Accounts will be drawn up to each _____.
5. The bankers shall be _____.
6. The partnership shall be dissolved on the expiry of not less than six months' notice of dissolution given in writing by one partner to the other or by any other mutually agreed procedure.
7. The partnership shall trade under the name of _____.
8. The net profits and losses shall be shared equally.
9. A partner may, from time to time, with the agreement of the other, be paid a salary prior to establishing the figure of net profit or loss for a particular year.

Signed: _____   Signed: _____

1.04 **The importance of a mission statement**

In the past we used to groan when it was suggested that every business should have a mission statement, but, as time has passed, this concept has become more widely accepted. Yes, I accept that it sounds like an American idea, but don't let's moan about and knock every idea that may come from the other side of the pond – and don't let's knock this one.

First of all, what is it? Well, mission statements are short, memorable and believable sentences that encapsulate what it is that your business stands for. I actually think they should be drafted in a way that the customers, as well as the employees, can read and, if they find they are true, accept.

Why have them? Because they summarise why you go to work. So often, people go to work simply to earn a crust. What I would like to see is people going to work to live; going to work to enjoy themselves, have fun and spread a little happiness each day both within their organisation and, more importantly, in the direction of their customers. Having a mission statement (at least having the right mission statement) can facilitate such an atmosphere.

You will probably be fed up with me harping on about my own experiences but it's these experiences that have given me the confidence to write this book – they are, I believe, important enough to share with you. In our business, we use the mission statement 'We want to score ten out of ten in everything we do for our clients'. We don't always achieve this score but, when we do, we get thank yous ('wows') accordingly.

This mission statement, which reflects our mission in our working life, is at the head of everyone's employment contract – if people don't believe it, they don't sign up to it and don't come to work for us. It's also measurable. We can ask our customers to rate us against this target, so we can tell how well or badly we're doing. It becomes a core belief and our reason for coming to work.

I happen to think that it's a particularly good one (not that I invented it, but the moment someone said it, I knew it was a winner) and you are welcome to use/plagiarise it.

But perhaps you can see that having a slogan like this provides a happy focus for everything you do at work, is easily remembered and, to counteract the criticisms of the moaners I mentioned at the start of this point, having a mission statement is actually rather a good idea.

1.05 **The importance of a vision statement**

A vision statement is a short (no more than one page) statement of what you want your business to look like in (say) five years' time.

Here is a typical template for you to develop in your own way. I've added some suggested words to fill the blanks:

Working vision statement

This firm has as its sole commercial purpose the objective of _____.

It will be acknowledged as the _best_ in its industry and region.

Team members will be _proud_ to be part of the firm and will benefit from _above_ average compensation, a _happy_ working environment, _constant_ opportunity for professional advancement and personal growth and _a close_ involvement in the decision-making process within the firm.

There will be a _high_ level of trust and mutual respect among all team members, owners and clients.

Each person _will_ understand and subscribe to the firm's mission and will _regularly_ assist in its accomplishment.

The owners of the firm will _always_ place the welfare of the firm and that of its clients above their own self-interests.

However, it will always be understood that the owners can expect to receive fair compensation reflecting the value of their contribution and the capital they have invested.

The firm will be innovative in its service delivery and will be guided by its principal purpose of _always wanting to excel_ .

The service it offers will be clearly defined, highly structured and priced in accordance to the value it represents to its clients.

2.01 **Investor's aspiration form**

How well are the intended participators going to work together?

We suggest that everyone takes a copy of this list and writes his answers down for an independent and knowledgeable person to review and report on how well it appears everyone will work together in the new business:

Name of person completing this form:	
Questions	**Answers**
What do I hope this business will achieve?	
Why do I think this business will be successful?	
What will I bring to the business in terms of opening capital for shares and any other assets?	
How much time will I devote to the business?	
What would I like to do in the business?	
What title would I like to have?	
What do I not want to do in the business?	
Who do I think the boss of the business should be?	
Will I be prepared to bring more money to the business should it be necessary to do so?	
When would I like to retire from the business?	
What do I hope to earn from the business each year?	
What dividends would I hope to be paid?	
What benefits would I like the business to provide? E.g. a car, mobile phone.	
What would I like to happen to my shares in the event of my early death?	
Who should sign cheques, etc.?	
Over what level of payment should a cheque have more than one signature?	
Where should the business bank?	
Should accounts be prepared more frequently than annually?	
Which firm of accountants should be appointed?	
Should there be a shareholders' agreement?	

Signed:_____Date:_____

Once the copies of these forms are complete, hand them to your chosen reviewer for him to look at, compare and then give his candid opinion of whether the people involved are likely to work well together, as well as to highlight where any potential difficulties appear to lie. The sort of person we have in mind to conduct this review might be a partner in the company's chosen firm of chartered accountants.

2.02 **Possible sources of finance**

- Your **family**
- Your **bank**
- **Leasing** (beware of the pitfalls) and **hire purchase**
- **Venture capital** – again there are pitfalls
- **Grants** – www.gov.uk, see below
- **Pension funds** and **insurance companies**
- **Others** – the list of individual organisations is very, very long.

Seeking government support

Borrowing money from a bank to start your business will be expensive and there are lots of tales of banks being 'fair weather' friends. Another source of finance could be a grant from the government to help with start-up costs.

Now, the government isn't in the business of giving grants to every small business that comes cap-in-hand to it. There are lots of factors (even limitations) that need to be adhered to.

Most grants are limited to the size of the business (in terms of employees). Location is also an important consideration and a grant may mean locating to another part of the country where special financial assistance is targeted.

Grants can be valuable, so it's worth checking through www.gov.uk. Its business helpline is 0845 600 9006 or go to the 'Business and self-employed' section of the website.

3.01 **Suggested terms of business**

What we enclose here is an example of the very minimum you should have. It should be available, or printed on the back of every invoice, and also included on your website.

As we have said before in this chapter, we strongly recommend you to take professional advice before you make your own terms of business public.

Here is some simple wording to get you started in a user-friendly way:

Thank you for using [*enter the name of your business*] for your purchase.

May we take a few moments to explain how we do business with our customers?

1. You may order products from us by telephone (01234 567890) or post (see the address below) or by email to sales@yourbusiness.com or through our website using PayPal.

2. When you pay by credit card you must be authorised to use the card you are charging.

3. Our prices include all postage costs within the UK.

4. All products are to be paid for prior to delivery, but see our two guarantees in the next two paragraphs.

5. We will deliver your order within 28 days. If we fail to meet this deadline, you are free to return the product, or cancel the purchase, and receive a full refund.

6. If having received any of our products you are not happy with any of them, send them back with original proof of purchase within 28 days to us at:

   Freepost (enter Freepost code)
   The name of your business
   Anytown
   Borsetshire
   AB20 7CD

   And we will send you a full no quibble refund.

7. If you have any complaints about our company, its employees or its products, please let us know and tell us how we can put the problem right.

3.02 **Non-disclosure agreement**

This Agreement is made on _____ by and between:

i)   Proposed collaborator (name) _____

and

ii)   Inventor's name _____

These people(s) will be referred to as 'the Parties'

Purpose of Agreement:

a)   The Parties will share certain information in order that each of them may consider establishing a business relationship for their mutual advantage.

b)   The Parties will define their rights with respect to the above information and both agree to protect the confidentiality thereof.

Both parties therefore agree as follows:

1.   Handling of Confidential Information, as defined in the Schedule to this Agreement

Each Party to this Agreement agrees:

i)   to keep confidential all information given by the other party, and to use such confidential information solely for the Purpose described above;

ii)   not to make any commercial use of the other Party's Confidential Information without their written permission;

iii)   not to use the Confidential Information for their, or any other person's benefit other than by further agreement with the other Party;

iv)   to keep the existence and nature of this Agreement confidential;

v)   not to disclose any related information with regard to this Agreement without the prior written consent of the other Party.

2.   Duration of Agreement

The obligations under the terms of this Agreement shall remain in effect for a period of XX years from the date hereof, and each Party hereby agrees that this term is reasonable and necessary.

3.   Return, and security, of Confidential Information

1.   Return

Each Party shall forthwith upon any request by the other:

a)   cease all use of the other Party's Confidential Information and promptly return such Confidential Information to such other Party and any other material passed or transmitted to it by the other Party pursuant to this Agreement and ensure the complete destruction of all such Confidential Information including computerised records in its possession or control; and

b)   provide a signed letter confirming that it has complied fully with this clause.

3.02 **Non-disclosure agreement** (continued)

All orally disclosed Confidential Information of the other Party shall continue to be held subject to the terms of this Agreement.

2. Security

    a) Each of the Parties undertakes to apply to all Confidential Information of the other Party no lesser security measures and degree of care than those which it applies to its own confidential or proprietary information.

    b) Each Party shall make copies of Confidential Information only to the extent that the same is strictly required for the Project.

    c) Each Party agrees to limit disclosure of the Confidential Information of the other Party to only those of its officers, employees and professional advisers who have a reasonable need to know the same for the Purpose.

4. Liability to possible damages

    Each Party agrees that its obligations under this Agreement are necessary and reasonable in order to protect the business interests of the other Party, and expressly acknowledges that monetary damages may well be inadequate to compensate the affected Party in the event of a breach of this Agreement. Accordingly both Parties agree and acknowledge that any such violation will cause irreparable injury to the Party whose Confidential Information is disclosed and that the Party so affected shall be entitled to obtain injunctive relief against the threatened or continued breach of this Agreement without the necessity of proving actual damages.

5. Effective dates

    All notices served under this Agreement shall be in writing and the date of service shall be deemed to be the day following the day on which the notice was posted.

Schedule of confidential information disclosed prior to the date of this Agreement

Description	Disclosing party

This Agreement has been signed on behalf of each Party by its duly authorised representative on the day and year above written.

Signed: _____   Signed: _____

For and on behalf of (name of proposed collaborator)

For and on behalf of (name of Inventor)

Authorised signatory

Authorised signatory

_____   _____

3.03 **Data protection recommendations**

For data security generally:

- Shred all your confidential paper waste.

- Check the physical security of your premises.

- Train your staff:

  a) so they know what is expected of them;

  b) to be wary of people who may try to trick them into giving out personal details;

  c) so that they can be prosecuted if they deliberately give out personal details without permission;

  d) to use a strong password – these are long (at least seven characters) and have a combination of upper- and lower-case letters, numbers and the special keyboard characters like the asterisk or currency symbols;

  e) not to send offensive emails about other people, their private lives or anything else that could bring your organisation into disrepute;

  f) not to believe emails that appear to come from your bank that ask for your account, credit card details or your password (a bank would never ask for this information in this way);

  g) not to open spam – not even to unsubscribe or ask for no more mailings. Tell them to delete the email and either get spam filters on your computers or use an email provider that offers this service.

For computer security:

- Install a firewall and virus-checking on your computers.

- Make sure that your operating system is set up to receive automatic updates.

- Protect your computer by downloading the latest patches or security updates, which should cover vulnerabilities.

- Only allow your staff access to the information they need to do their job and don't let them share passwords.

- Encrypt any personal information held electronically that would cause damage or distress if it were lost or stolen.

- Take regular back-ups of the information on your computer system and keep them in a separate place so that if you lose your computers, you don't lose the information.

- Securely remove all personal information before disposing of old computers (by using technology or destroying the hard disk).

- Consider installing an anti-spyware tool. Spyware is the generic name given to programs that are designed to secretly monitor your activities on your computer. Spyware can be unwittingly installed within other file and program downloads, and their use is often malicious. They can capture passwords, banking credentials and credit card details, and then relay them back to fraudsters. Anti-spyware helps to monitor and protect your computer from spyware threats, and it is often free to use and update.

3.03 **Data protection recommendations** (continued)

For using emails securely:

- Consider whether the content of the email should be encrypted or password protected. Your IT or security team should be able to assist you with encryption.

- When you start to type in the name of the recipient, some email software will suggest similar addresses you have used before. If you have previously emailed several people whose name or address starts the same way – for example 'Dave' – the auto-complete function may bring up several 'Daves'. Make sure you choose the right address before you click send.

- If you want to send an email to a recipient without revealing his address to other recipients, make sure you use blind carbon copy (bcc), not carbon copy (cc). When you use cc every recipient of the message will be able to see the address it was sent to.

- Be careful when using a group email address. Check who is in the group and make sure you really want to send your message to everyone.

- If you send a sensitive email from a secure server to an insecure recipient, security will be threatened. You may need to check that the recipient's arrangements are secure enough before sending your message.

For using faxes securely:

- Consider whether sending the information by a means other than fax is more appropriate, such as using a courier service or secure email. Make sure you only send the information that is required. For example, if a solicitor asks you to forward a statement, send only the statement specifically asked for, not all statements available on the file.

- Make sure you double-check the fax number you are using. It is best to dial from a directory of previously verified numbers.

- Check that you are sending a fax to a recipient with adequate security measures in place. For example, your fax should not be left uncollected in an open-plan office.

- If the fax is sensitive, ask the recipient to confirm that he is at the fax machine, he is ready to receive the document, and there is sufficient paper in the machine.

- Ring up or email to make sure the whole document has been received safely.

- Use a cover sheet. This will let anyone know who the information is for and whether it is confidential or sensitive, without him having to look at the contents.

3.04 **Fire safety risk assessment**

Suggested checklist for use when carrying out a fire risk assessment:

- When did you last carry out a fire risk assessment?
- Have you found anything that could start a fire?
- Have you found anything that could burn?
- Which people are at risk?
- Have you assessed the risk of a fire at your workplace and its impact on the safety of your employees and visitors?
- Have you kept sources of fuel and sparks apart?
- Have you made any fuel secure?

In case of fire:

- Will you/your people know there is a fire?
- Do you have a plan to warn others?
- Who will make sure everyone gets out?
- Who will call the fire brigade?

Fire precautions:

- What equipment do you have on your premises to extinguish a small fire yourself?
- Have you planned escape routes?
- Does everyone know the fire escape routes?
- Does your safety equipment work?
- When was it last tested?
- Do your people know how to use the fire safety equipment?
- Do they know where it is?
- Have you discussed this issue with the staff?
- If you are using this checklist annually, have there been any changes since the last check (to the building, work premises or practices, etc.) that need to be given special consideration?
- What date will you have your next fire risk assessment? Have you made a diary note to remember to do this?

3.05 **Suggested shareholders' agreement**

> If you are going into business by owning shares in a limited company with others, you should seriously consider signing a shareholders' agreement, whereby you agree, at the outset, a whole range of important issues. This agreement should be drawn up after you've all been through the exercise of preparing the investor's aspiration form.
>
> The following draft isn't intended to represent any document that you may decide to sign, but it will give you the flavour of what a shareholders' agreement should contain. In other words, it will be full of legalese, so be prepared; in my view, the most important document to agree on is the investor's aspiration form.

SHAREHOLDERS' AGREEMENT

Concerning the shareholders of

_____Ltd

('the Company').

THIS AGREEMENT is made the [*date*] day of January [*year*].

BETWEEN the following shareholders/parties:

1) _____

2) _____

3) _____

Background:

A) The Company was incorporated under the Companies Act 1985 on [*date*] and currently has an authorised share capital of £[*amount*] divided into [*number*] ordinary shares of £1 each of which [*number*] have been issued at par.

B) The Parties have agreed to co-operate in the establishment and management of the business of [*enter company name*] through the medium of the Company.

C) The Shareholders have agreed to subscribe for shares in the capital of the Company upon the terms and conditions hereinafter appearing.

D) The Parties have agreed to enter into this Agreement for the purpose of regulating their relationship with each other and certain aspects of the affairs of and their dealings with the Company.

NOW THIS AGREEMENT ESTABLISHES THE FOLLOWING:

1. Interpretation

In this Agreement and the Recitals, except where the context states otherwise, the following expressions shall have the following meanings:

'in the Agreed Proportions' – means [*number*] per cent in respect of [*name*] and [*number*] per cent in respect of [*name*].

'in the Agreed Terms' – means 'in the form of an annexed draft agreed between the parties or their respective legal advisers'.

3.05 **Suggested shareholders' agreement** (continued)

'Board' – means in the Board of Directors for the time being of the Company.

'Business' – means the business of the Company as described in Recital B and such other business as the Shareholders may agree from time to time in writing should be carried on by the Company.

'Director' – means any director for the time being of the Company including where applicable any alternate director.

'Equity Share Capital' – shall have the meaning ascribed to such expression by Section 744 of the Companies Act 1985.

'Party' – means a party to this Agreement.

'Person' – means an association or a body corporated or unincorporated or a partnership and 'Persons' shall be construed accordingly.

'Shareholders' – means together and/or any Person or Persons to whom they may properly transfer their Shares pursuant to the provisions of this Agreement.

'Shares' – means shares in the share capital of the Company.

'Taxes Act' – means the Income and Corporation Taxes Act 1988.

2. **Objects of the Company**

The primary object of the Company shall be to carry on the business of [*enter aims*].

The Business shall be conducted in the best interest of the Company on sound commercial profit making principles so as to generate the maximum achievable maintainable profits available for distribution and as varied from time to time by agreement in writing between the Shareholders.

3. **Completion**

Forthwith, or as soon as practicable after executing this Agreement but before the Company commences trading, each of the Shareholders shall take or cause to be taken the following steps at Directors' and Shareholders' meetings of the Company (as appropriate):

- The adoption by the Company of new Articles of Association in the Agreed Terms.

- The appointment of [*enter name*] as an 'A' Director of the Company.

- The subscription by [*enter name*] for [*enter number*] Shares of £1 each in the Company at par and the allotment and issue of such shares by the Company to [*enter name*] against payment in full in cash.

- The subscription by [*enter amount*] for [*enter number*] Shares of £1 each in the Company at par and the allotment and issue of such shares by the Company to [*enter name*] against payment in full in cash.

4. **Appointment of Directors**

The maximum number of Directors holding office at any time shall be [*enter number*] unless otherwise expressly agreed in writing by each of the Shareholders.

- Each of the Shareholders shall be entitled to appoint themselves as Directors.

- Board Meetings shall be held [*give frequency*] and, unless otherwise agreed by the Shareholders, seven days' notice shall be given to each of the Directors of all meetings of the Board. Each such notice shall contain an agenda specifying in reasonable detail the matters

3.05 **Suggested shareholders' agreement** (continued)

to be discussed at the relevant meeting and shall be accompanied by any relevant papers for discussion at such meeting. The quorum for Board Meetings shall be two Directors.

- The Chairman of the meeting of the Board shall not be entitled to a second or a casting vote.

5. Conduct of the Company's affairs

The Shareholders shall exercise all voting rights and other powers of control available to them in relation to the Company so as to procure (insofar as they are able by the exercise of such rights and powers) that at all times during the term of this Agreement:

[*Enter details*]

6. Matters requiring consent of the Shareholders

The Shareholders shall exercise all voting rights and other powers of control available to them in relation to the Company so as to procure (insofar as they are able by the exercise of such rights and powers) that neither the Company nor any Subsidiary of the Company shall, without the prior written consent of both of the Shareholders (for the avoidance of doubt approved minutes of any Board or Shareholders' Meeting shall be evidence of such written consent):

- create any fixed or floating charge, lien (other than a lien arising by operation of law) or other encumbrance over the whole or any part of the undertaking, property or assets of the Company or of such Subsidiary, except for the purpose of securing the indebtedness of the Company to its bankers for sums borrowed in the ordinary and proper course of the Business;

- borrow any sum of money (except from the Company's bankers in the ordinary and proper course of the Business) in excess of a maximum aggregate sum outstanding at any time of £[*insert*];

- make any loan or advance or give any credit (other than normal trade credit) in excess of £[*insert*] to any Person, except for the purpose of making deposits with bankers which shall be repayable upon the giving of no more than seven days' notice.

7. Staff

The Company shall recruit and employ staff as the Board shall from time to time consider necessary.

8. Working capital

The Shareholders shall each use reasonable endeavours to procure the requirements of the Company for working capital to finance the Business.

9. Guarantees given by the Shareholders

Neither of the Shareholders will be required to give any guarantees in relation to the Company at any time during the term of this Agreement.

10. Disposal or charging of the shares

Neither of the Shareholders shall, except with the prior written consent of the other, dispose or pledge (create a charge) over all or any of the Shares held by them.

Suggested shareholders' agreement (continued)

11. Issue of shares

The issue of new Shares shall be regulated in accordance with the provisions set out in the Company's Articles of Association.

12. Transfer of shares

The transfer of Shares shall be regulated in accordance with the provisions set out in the Company's Articles of Association.

13. Exercise of voting rights

Each Shareholder undertakes with the other generally to use his best endeavours to promote the Business and the interests of the Company.

14. Procedure in the event of deadlock

In any case of deadlock each of the Shareholders shall, within seven days of such deadlock having arisen or become apparent, prepare and circulate to the other Shareholder and other Directors a memorandum or other form of statement setting out his position on the matter in dispute and his reasons for adopting such a position.

If a resolution or disposition is not agreed within 30 days after delivery of the memorandum or statement mentioned therein, either of the Shareholders ('the Buyer') may serve on the other Shareholder a notice in writing ('a Deadlock Notice') offering to purchase all of the Shares held by the Seller ('the Sale Shares').

The Deadlock Notice shall specify the price at which the Buyer is prepared to buy the Sale Shares from the Seller ('the Deadlock Price') but shall not include any other condition whatsoever.

15. Duration

This Agreement shall continue in full force and effect until the first to occur of the following dates:

- the date of commencement of the Company's winding up; or
- the date on which the Shareholders agree in writing to terminate this Agreement.

16. Previous Agreements

This Agreement supersedes any previous agreement made between the Parties in relation to the matters dealt with herein and represents the entire understanding between the parties in relation thereto.

17. The terms of this agreement to prevail

In the event of any ambiguity or conflict arising between the terms of this Agreement and those of the Company's Memorandum and Articles of Association, the terms of this Agreement shall prevail as between the Shareholders.

IN WITNESS whereof the Parties hereto have duly executed this Agreement the day and year first before written.

Signed by the parties: _____

_____

3.06 **Business names – what to do**

Every business is legally obliged to display their business name – and other details – to inform customers and suppliers who they are dealing with.

DISPLAYING A LIMITED COMPANY NAME (This also applies to limited liability partnerships (LLPs))

You must display a sign at your place of business that shows your company name. It must be easily read, be clearly visible and always on display – not just during business hours.

You must also include the registered name on all letters, faxes, business cards and business communications, as well as on email and other correspondence and on your website (see also below).

You must also show the place of registration, the registered number, the address of the registered office, and the fact that it is a limited company or LLP.

You do not have to state directors' names on business letters unless you want to do so. However, if you do decide to include directors' names, then you must state all the directors' names.

DISPLAYING A SOLE TRADER OR PARTNERSHIP BUSINESS NAME

If you are a sole trader or partnership, you must display a sign at your place of business that shows your business name. It must be easily read, be clearly visible and always on display – not just during business hours.

Your business name, your own name and business address must be clearly displayed on all letters, faxes, business cards and business communications, as well as on email and other correspondence and on your website (see also below).

If you decide to display the partners' names, then all the names must be included.

THE FORMAL WAY OF DISPLAYING YOUR NAME

One way of displaying your name is to use the proforma sheet on the following page, a larger version of which is available from the publishers, Lawpack.

DISPLAYING ANY NAME ONLINE

If your business has a website, you must display:

*   General information about your business – including business name, address, telephone and fax numbers, email address, VAT registration number (if applicable)
*   Details of any relevant professional body that you belong to.

Notice of particulars of ownership

Notice of Particulars of Ownership

As required by Section 1202 of the Companies Act 2006

_____

Insert name of business

Proprietor

_____

Insert full name of business proprietor

Address within Great Britain at which documents relating to the business may
be effectively served on the proprietor

_____
_____
_____
_____
_____

Insert full address

3.08 **Business stationery – what it must show**

All business stationery, order forms, emails, websites, etc. must include the following information:

*   The company name, including the word 'limited'
*   The place of its registration (England and Wales, Scotland or Northern Ireland)
*   Its registered number
*   The address of its registered office.

In addition it's also sensible to include:

*   Its address, if it's not the same as the registered office
*   Contact details such as website, phone and fax numbers, etc.
*   VAT number, if appropriate.

If the names of directors are included, then all of the names must be printed. It's unwise to print the names of all directors because if one ceases to act, it will necessitate the reprinting of all business stationery.

An investment company must state that it is one on its stationery.

4.01 **Suggested job application form**

Job application for work at_____

PERSONAL DETAILS			
Surname:		Date of birth:	
Forename(s):		Age last birthday:	
Address:		Marital status:	
		Children (give ages):	
Telephone (home):			
Telephone (office):		Do you hold a current full driving licence?	

EDUCATION			
From	To	Name and address of school/ college/university	Examinations passed (including grades)

OTHER RELEVANT COURSES TAKEN			
From	To	Course organiser	Title/Subject

4.01 **Suggested job application form** (continued)

MEMBERSHIP OF PROFESSIONAL INSTITUTIONS		
Date obtained	Grade	Institution

EMPLOYMENT HISTORY				
From	To	Employer's name and address	Position held	Reason for leaving

REFERENCES

Please give name, occupation, address and daytime telephone number of your last three employers (or personal referee if this is not applicable). The applicant's present employer will not be approached without the applicant's prior consent.

1)	2)	3)

4.01 **Suggested job application form** (continued)

EXPERIENCE AND ABILITIES

What experience, abilities and skills do you have which you feel might be relevant to the position applied for? Please append additional sheets if necessary.

HOBBIES AND INTERESTS

Give a brief summary of your recreational activities.

OTHER

Have you any court, court-martial, conviction, outstanding summons or prosecution (except spent convictions under the Rehabilitation of Offenders Act 1974)? If yes, please give details.

DECLARATION

The information given by me on this form is correct in every detail.

Signed: _____

Date: _____

4.02 **Questionnaire to help you decide if an employee can be treated as self-employed**

HMRC are keen to classify self-employed people as employees because this increases National Insurance Contributions and Income Tax.

How can you tell if someone is an employee or is self-employed? Answering the following questions should help. Note that there are separate and new rules for workers in the construction industry; the following questions are not appropriate for such workers. (On the HMRC website there is an Employment Status Indicator that can be used as a guide, although it may still be worthwhile getting professional advice on the matter.)

1.	Is there a contract of service, i.e. a contract of employment? *A 'no' answer indicates self-employment.*	☐ YES ☐ NO
2.	Is there a contract for services, i.e. a notice supplied by the person carrying out the work (A), indicating the nature of goods or services he will provide to B (this need not be written)? *A 'yes' answer indicates self-employment.*	☐ YES ☐ NO
3.	Is the person who does the work in business on his own account? *A 'yes' answer indicates self-employment.*	☐ YES ☐ NO
4.	If the person is in business on his own account, has evidence been provided that this is indeed the case (e.g. copy accounts, the payment of Class 2 National Insurance Contributions)? *A 'yes' answer indicates self-employment.*	☐ YES ☐ NO
5.	Are the hours worked decided by the person doing the work? *A 'yes' answer indicates self-employment.*	☐ YES ☐ NO
6.	Are the days worked decided by the person doing the work? *A 'yes' answer indicates self-employment.*	☐ YES ☐ NO
7.	Does the person doing the work decide when to take his own holidays? *A 'yes' answer indicates self-employment.*	☐ YES ☐ NO
8.	Does the business proprietor supervise the work? *A 'no' answer indicates self-employment.*	☐ YES ☐ NO
9.	Is the person part and parcel of the business? *A 'no' answer indicates self-employment.*	☐ YES ☐ NO
10.	Does the person supply tools and/or materials when he carries out the work? *A 'yes' answer indicates self-employment.*	☐ YES ☐ NO
11.	Does the person doing the work give the business an invoice for the work done? *A 'yes' answer indicates self-employment.*	☐ YES ☐ NO

4.02 **Questionnaire to help you decide if an employee can be treated as self-employed** (continued)

12. Does the business calculate how much to pay the person doing the work and give a payslip? *A 'no' answer indicates self-employment.*	☐ YES ☐ NO
13. Is self-employment the intention of both parties? *A 'yes' answer indicates self-employment.*	☐ YES ☐ NO
14. Is the person bound by the customer care credo of the business? *A 'no' answer indicates self-employment.*	☐ YES ☐ NO
15. Is the person carrying out the work required to wear a uniform or dress tidily at the diktat of the business? *A 'no' answer indicates self-employment.*	☐ YES ☐ NO
16. Is the person carrying out the work provided with a car or transport by the business? *A 'no' answer indicates self-employment.*	☐ YES ☐ NO
17. In the event of sickness, does the business continue to pay the person while not at work? *A 'no' answer indicates self-employment.*	☐ YES ☐ NO
18. Is the person carrying out the work at liberty to work for other businesses? *A 'yes' answer indicates self-employment.*	☐ YES ☐ NO
19. Is the person carrying out the work required to work in order to perform a specific task? *A 'yes' answer indicates self-employment.*	☐ YES ☐ NO
20. Does the business, on asking this person to carry out work for them, assume any responsibility or liability characteristic of an employment, e.g. employment protection, employees' liability, pension entitlements, etc.? *A 'no' answer indicates self-employment.*	☐ YES ☐ NO
21. Is the person who does the work paid an agreed price per job? *A 'yes' answer indicates self-employment (i.e. he is not paid for the hours he works, but for the work carried out).*	☐ YES ☐ NO
22. Is the work carried out regularly? *A 'no' answer indicates self-employment.*	☐ YES ☐ NO
23. Does the individual work for other people? *A 'yes' answer indicates self-employment.*	☐ YES ☐ NO
24. Does the person carrying out the work advertise? *A 'yes' answer indicates self-employment.*	☐ YES ☐ NO

4.02 **Questionnaire to help you decide if an employee can be treated as self-employed** (continued)

25.	Does the person carrying out the work have headed stationery?	☐ YES ☐ NO
	A 'yes' answer indicates self-employment.	
26.	Can the person send a substitute? If so, has this ever happened?	☐ YES ☐ NO
	A 'yes' answer indicates self-employment.	
27.	Does the person have to rectify faulty workmanship in his own time and at his own expense?	☐ YES ☐ NO
	A 'yes' answer indicates self-employment.	

Having addressed these questions, you should now begin to know whether in reality the person under consideration is an employee or is self-employed. However, a definite answer can only be given by the courts and just because a worker is self-employed elsewhere he can still be classed as an employee of yours.

4.03 **Suggested plan for interviewing a new member of staff**

1. Give a full job description in the advertisement.

2. Prepare a profile of the ideal candidate:

   a) Background

   b) Experience

   c) Qualifications.

   For internal use only, not for the candidate to see

3. Send candidate:

   a) Letter inviting to interview

   b) Date, time and place of interview (and send directions)

   c) An application form – this saves the interviewer a lot of time because each candidate's details will be laid out consistently.

4. Tell reception names of candidates attending.

5. Prepare for interview – have completed application form in front of you.

   Have certain questions to ask each candidate:

   a) Questions that relate to the job: 'Describe your experience in this field'.

   b) Questions that relate to the candidate – i.e. to find out his good and weak points. Test his honesty. Get him to talk about:

   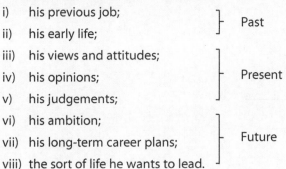

   i) his previous job;

   ii) his early life;

   Past

   iii) his views and attitudes;

   iv) his opinions;

   v) his judgements;

   Present

   vi) his ambition;

   vii) his long-term career plans;

   viii) the sort of life he wants to lead.

   Future

   Tell the candidate what will happen after the interview – i.e. when he will be told how he got on. (If it is certain he has not got the job he should be told there and then.)

   Probe all gaps in the applicant's record.

   Ask to see qualifications.

6. As soon as the interview is over write down assessment.

7. The receptionist should ask what he is owed for expenses.

8. The decision should be made promptly and swiftly notified.

4.04 **Letter not calling job applicant to interview**

Dear _____

POSITION OF _____

Thank you for your application for the above position.

Unfortunately, on this occasion, you have not been selected for an interview. However, we will keep your details on file for six months and contact you if any other suitable vacancy arises.

I would like to take this opportunity to thank you for your interest you have shown in our company, and wish you every success for the future.

Yours sincerely

_____

4.05 **Letter calling job applicant to interview**

Dear _____

POSITION OF _____

Thank you for your application for the above position within our company.

I am pleased to advise that you have been selected to attend a first interview at _____on _____.
Please report to [*give address*].

If you have any difficulties attending the meeting, please call the undersigned to re-arrange a more convenient time.

We do/do not intend paying for your travel expenses.

I look forward to meeting you.

Yours sincerely

_____

4.06 **Suggested format for interview notes**

Applicant's name:	
Position applied for:	

1	Physical appearance/Impression given

2	Qualifications already achieved/Education

3	Work experience/Continuity of employment

4	Skills relevant to job (Strengths)

5	What further training/Qualification will be required

6	Current salary/Expected salary/Benefits

4.06 **Suggested format for interview notes** (continued)

Applicant's name:	
Position applied for:	
Date of interview:	

Impressions gained	Scores out of ten
Initial impression	
Impression by the end	
Presentation	
Communications (Verbal)	
Communications (Written)	
Keyboard skills	
Computer literacy	
Organisational skills	
Good time management	
Innovative/Creative	
Team worker	
Managing others	
Financial awareness	
Attention to detail	
Drive/Self-confidence	
Relevant work experience in previous position	

4.07 **Letter offering job**

Dear _____

Re: [*Job title*]
        [*Company address*]

I am delighted to confirm that you have been successful in your application for the above post and write to confirm the company's offer of employment.

Your starting salary will be £_____ per annum.

If you accept this offer of employment, your employment will commence on [*enter date*]. Our offices/place of business opens at 9.00am but please arrive at (say) 9.30am on your first day of work.

The first three months of your employment will be a trial period, during which time your employment may be terminated by us or by you on one week's notice.

Your normal hours of work will be 9.00am to 5.30pm, Monday to Friday. Holiday entitlement will be twenty days per annum, five of which will be stipulated by the company.

The full terms and conditions of employment are set out in your contract of employment and the company's Staff Handbook.

The offer is subject to receipt by the company of the following:

• Satisfactory references (unless you object, I shall contact the referees nominated on your application form immediately)

• A copy of a suitable identity document.

I look forward to receiving your acceptance and confirmation of your starting date. In the meantime, if you have any queries, please do not hesitate to telephone me.

Yours sincerely

_____

4.08 **New employee details**

Personal details

Name	
Address	
Date of birth	
Maiden name	
Date of marriage	
Date joined	
Job title	
N.I. number	
N.I. code	
Contract issued (Yes/No)	
How paid (Hourly/Salaried)	
Holiday entitlement	
Any benefits	
Any deductions	
Long-term ambitions	

Emergency contact
(Please tell us whom we should contact in an emergency, e.g. if you were taken ill.)

Title	
Forename(s)	
Surname	
Relationship to you	
Home telephone number	
Work telephone number	
Mobile telephone number	

4.09 **Letter following failed interview**

Dear _____

POSITION OF _____

Thank you for attending the interview for the above position. The high calibre of applicants interviewed has made the selection extremely difficult and unfortunately, on this occasion, you have not been successful in your application. The company will hold your details on file and will contact you again if any suitable openings arise during the next six months.

I would like to take this opportunity of thanking you for the time and interest you have shown in the company and to wish you success with your future career.

Yours sincerely

_____

4.10 **Template contract of employment**

Reproduced here for guidance is Lawpack's template employment contract, which contains standard terms. Professional advice should be sought according to the requirements of employers.

FULL-TIME/PART-TIME EMPLOYMENT CONTRACT
ENGLAND & WALES

THIS AGREEMENT IS MADE the _____ day of _____ 20 _____

BETWEEN **(1)** _____ of _____

_____ (the 'Employer');

and

(2) _____ of _____

_____ (the 'Employee').

This document sets out the terms and conditions of employment which are required to be given to the Employee under section 1 Employment Rights Act 1996 and which apply at the date hereof.

1. COMMENCEMENT AND JOB TITLE. The Employer agrees to employ the Employee from _____ year____ in the capacity of _____at _____ .

    [No employment with a previous employer will be counted as part of the Employee's period of continuous employment.] [The employment under this Agreement forms part of a continuous period of employment which began on _____.]

    [The Employee's duties which the job entails are set out in the job description attached to this statement.] The Employee's duties [as set out in the attached job description] may from time to time be reasonably modified as necessary to meet the needs of the Employer's business.

2. SALARY. The Employer shall pay the Employee a salary of £ _____ per year by equal [weekly] [monthly] instalments in arrears.

3. HOURS OF EMPLOYMENT. The Employee's normal hours of employment shall be _____ to _____ on _____ [and _____ to _____ on Saturdays] during which time the Employee may take up to one hour for lunch between the hours of 12pm and 2pm, and the Employee may from time to time be required to work such additional hours as is reasonable to meet the requirements of the Employer's business [at no additional payment] [at an overtime rate of £ _____ per hour].

4. HOLIDAYS. The Employee shall be entitled to _____ days' holiday per calendar year at full pay in addition to the normal public holidays. Holidays must be taken at a time that is convenient to the Employer and no more than _____ weeks' holiday may be taken at any one time.

5. SICKNESS. The Employee shall be paid normal remuneration during sickness absence for a maximum of _____ weeks in any period of twelve months provided that the Employee provides the Employer with a medical certificate in the case of absence of more than seven consecutive days. Such remuneration will be less the amount of any Statutory Sick Pay or Social Security sickness benefits to which the Employee may be entitled.

6. COLLECTIVE AGREEMENTS. [There are no collective agreements in force directly relating to the terms of your employment.] [The terms of the collective agreement dated _____ made between _____ and _____ shall be deemed to be included in this Agreement.]

7. PENSION. [There is no pension scheme applicable to the Employee.] [The Employee shall be entitled to join the Employer's pension scheme the details of which are set out in the Employer's booklet/leaflet entitled _____ _____ which is available on request.] A contracting-out certificate under the Pension Schemes Act 1993 [is][is not] in force in respect of this employment.

8. TERMINATION. The Employer may terminate this Agreement by giving written notice to the Employee as follows:

    (a) with not less than one week's notice during the first two years of continuous employment;

    (b) with not less than one week's notice for each full year of continuous employment after the first two years until the twelfth year of continuous employment; and

    (c) with not less than twelve weeks' notice after twelve years of continuous employment.

4.10 **Template contract of Employment** (continued)

The Employer may terminate this Agreement without notice or payment in lieu of notice in the case of serious or persistent misconduct such as to cause a major breach of the Employer's disciplinary rules.

The Employee may terminate this Agreement by one week's written notice to the Employer.

9. CONFIDENTIALITY. The Employee is aware that during his/her employment he/she may be party to confidential information concerning the Employer and the Employer's business. The Employee shall not during the term of this employment disclose or allow the disclosure of any confidential information (except in the proper course of his/her employment). After the termination of this Agreement the Employee shall not disclose or use any of the Employer's trade secrets or any other information which is of a sufficiently high degree of confidentiality to amount to a trade secret. The Employer shall be entitled to apply for an injunction to prevent such disclosure or use and to seek any other remedy including without limitation the recovery of damages in the case of such disclosure or use.

10. NON-COMPETITION. For a period of [_____ months] [_____year(s)] after the termination of this Agreement the Employee shall not solicit or seek business from any customers or clients of the Employer who were customers or clients of the Employer at any time during the _____ years immediately preceding the termination of this Agreement.

11. DISMISSAL, DISCIPLINE AND GRIEVANCE. The Employer's Dismissal and Disciplinary Rules and Procedure and the Grievance and Appeal Procedure in connection with these rules are set out in the Employer's Staff Handbook a copy of which is attached hereto.

12. NOTICES. All communications including notices required to be given under this Agreement shall be in writing and shall be sent either by personal service or first class post to the Parties' respective addresses.

13. SEVERABILITY. If any provision of this Agreement should be held to be invalid it shall to that extent be severed and the remaining provisions shall continue to have full force and effect.

14. ENTIRE AGREEMENT. [Other than the Staff Handbook as amended from time to time [and Working Time Regulations Opt Out Agreement] which form[s] part of the Employee's Contract,] [t][T]his Agreement contains the entire Agreement between the Parties and supersedes all prior arrangements and understandings whether written or oral with respect to the subject matter hereof and may not be varied except in writing signed by both the Parties hereto.

15. GOVERNING LAW. This Agreement shall be construed in accordance with the laws of England and Wales and shall be subject to the exclusive jurisdiction of the English courts.

IN WITNESS OF WHICH the parties hereto have signed this Agreement the day and year first above written.

SIGNED _____

Signed by or on behalf of the Employer   in the presence of (witness)

Name _____

Address _____

_____

DATED _____   Occupation _____

SIGNED _____

Signed by the Employee   in the presence of (witness)

Name _____

Address _____

_____

DATED _____   Occupation _____

4.11 **Suggested matters for staff handbook**

NAME OF EMPLOYER

It is suggested that this document includes matters such as the following, which are included in Lawpack's Staff Handbook, available at www.lawpack.co.uk:

Equal Opportunities Policy
Health and Safety Policy
Training
Business Expenses
Attendance and Timekeeping
Appearance
Drug and Alcohol Misuse Policy
Smoking
Use of Email and the Internet
Use of Telephones and Other Facilities
Acceptance of Gifts
Data Protection Policy
Maternity, Paternity, Adoption and Parental Leave Policy
Flexible Working Policy
Time Off for Dependants
Sickness Absence Policy
Whistleblowing Policy
Disciplinary and Dismissal Procedure
Grievance Procedure
Redundancy Procedure

- 2 -

4.12 **Letter asking for a reference**

PRIVATE AND CONFIDENTIAL

Dear _____

RE: _____

We have recently interviewed the above candidate for the position of _____ with this company and would be grateful if you could provide a reference on our attached reference form.

Please return the reference to us in the enclosed stamped-addressed envelope. An early reply would be very much appreciated.

If you have any queries in this matter, please do not hesitate to telephone. May I take this opportunity of thanking you for your assistance in this matter.

Yours sincerely

_____

4.12 **Letter asking for a reference** (continued)

Reference request

All information is treated in confidence. Please return the completed form in the enclosed stamped-addressed envelope.

Applicant's name:	
Position held:	
Company:	
Date employment began:	
Date employment ended:	
Position applied for:	
Company:	

Please tick the appropriate box:	V. Good	Good	Average	Poor
1. Time keeping/Sickness record				
2. Appearance				
3. Behaviour and attitude				
4. Work relationships				
5. Organisational skills				
6. Initiative, creativity				
7. Problem solving				
8. Accuracy in work				
9. Communication skills – written and verbal				
10. Other: Should there be a category you would like to mention				
11. Is there any issue you would like to address? Please do so here or overleaf.				
12. Please would you write a brief summary giving your views on the candidate's suitability for the above mentioned post.				

PLEASE CONTINUE OVERLEAF IF NECESSARY

Signed: _____ Position: _____ Date: _____

4.13 **Employee appraisal form**

We aim to improve our business performance by helping you develop your personal skills. So once a year we need to assess the progress we have both made in this regard.

1.	Do you feel you have improved since the last review?*	
2.	If you have improved, please describe the improvement.	
3.	What main difficulties did you have during the period in achieving this improvement?	
4.	Are there any key responsibilities in your job description (attached) that are no longer appropriate?	
5.	Are there any key responsibilities that should be added?	
6.	What skills and abilities do you have that are not being made use of in your job?	
7.	Are there any changes that could be made by the partners, yourself, other people to help you improve your performance?	
8.	Are there any objectives you would like to achieve in the next six months?	
9.	Is there any further training and development we could provide that could help you to achieve your objectives?	
10.	How would you like to see your job developing within the firm?	
11.	What suggestions do you have for making the firm a more satisfying place in which to work?	
12.	Do you have any other matters you would like to discuss?	

*If the answer is 'no' then we can discuss this at the meeting.

Please let me have this form completed before the meeting.

Signed: _____ Employer

4.14 **Suggested holiday form**

Holidays (days)

Holiday year from 1 January 201 _____ to 31 December 201 _____

Name:_____ Holiday entitlement:_____

Period applied for (inclusive dates)		Number of days applied for	Total number of days taken including days now applied for	Number of days left	Office records	
From	To				Partner's initials	Date approved

Time off in lieu (hours)

Extra hours worked			Time being reclaimed		Unclaimed hours remaining	Office records	
Date	Client/ Reason, etc.	Number of hours	Date	Number	Number	Partner's initials	Date approved

4.15 **Sample agreement when one spouse works for another**

It is not uncommon for one spouse to employ the other but for the payments, being of a modest nature, to not be subject to income tax or National Insurance but, nonetheless, HMRC may challenge the payments as not being properly paid in accordance with the rules for normal business expenditure.

Accordingly it is as well to (as the saying goes) "do the thing properly" and for both spouses to sign a sensible agreement.

Such an agreement might be worded thus:

AGREEMENT BETWEEN

_____

AND

_____

We, the undersigned, agree that my wife / husband / etc undertakes responsibility for the following activities in my business:

1. _____

2. _____

3. _____

4. _____

5. _____

6. _____

It is agreed that, for these services, he/she will receive the sum of £_____* per year to be paid monthly.

This agreement is effective from_____

Signed _____Proprietor

Signed _____Spouse

Date _____

*You might need to take professional advice to be sure that the level of pay chosen does not lead to any tax etc., liabilities.

4.16 **What records does an employer have to keep?**

It has often struck us as strange that there is no complete and all-embracing PAYE recording system that you can buy in a stationery shop. We ourselves have often considered devising such a system to help employers fulfil their obligations, but, to date, this has not been achieved.

A proper system for keeping employees' records would consist of the following:

For each employee:

- A contract of employment
- Notices of PAYE coding
- A permanent record sheet which would record the employee's name, date of birth, National Insurance number, date of joining, dates of pay rises, etc.

But, in addition, you would need to keep properly filed away HMRC's instructions for employers:

- Table A
- Table B
- National Insurance instructions for employers
- National Insurance tables
- Pension fund details
  Etc.

In other words, employers certainly have a number of important obligations. Our view is that, if employers are doing their job properly, they will want to keep their records properly, pay their people properly and keep within the law. In our experience it's businesses that behave in such a manner that succeed and flourish.

4.17 **Sample job description**

It would not be appropriate for this book to provide draft job descriptions, but here are a few headings for you to consider:

Name of Employer _____

Name of Employee _____

Job Title _____

Reporting to _____

(Give the title(s) of the appropriate manager(s).)

Key purpose of the job _____

Main duties and responsibilities

1. _____

2. _____

3. _____

This job description was reviewed (and amended by agreement) on_____

4.18 Employee travel expense and/or mileage claim

Name of Employer_____

Name of Employee _____

Department_____

Date	Reason for travel	Mileage travelled	Mileage expense claimed	Other expenses incurred	
				Description	Total claimed
Total mileage expense claimed			£	Total other expense	£
Transfer mileage expense total to right hand column					£
Grand total expense claim					£

_____

Agreed by Partner/ Manager / Director (Name and sign)

_____

Date paid

4.19 **Plan for weekly management get together with individual member of staff**

Suggest no more than 10 minutes

Name of staff _____

Department _____

Suggested questions	Space for answers
What have you been working on?	
What's your week been like?	
How are things with the family?	
Should you update me on anything?	
Are you on track to complete the job on time?	
Do you need any assistance in terms of instruction?	
Extra help?	
Is there any way in which I might be more helpful to you?	
What worries do you have?	
Do you have any suggestions I might take on board?	
Other comments	

_____

Signed

_____

Date

4.20 **Employee contact details – suggested layout**

London Office

First Name	Last Name	Job Title	Specific Responsibilities	Office Number	Mobile	Email

Regional Office

Directors

Main Customers

Main Suppliers

4.21 **Additional suggested report of employee details**

This can be very useful for new employees and visitors to your premises

Head Office

| PHOTO | Manager _____ | PHOTO | Assistant _____ |

Reception

| PHOTO | Manager _____ | PHOTO | Assistant _____ |

Sales

| PHOTO | Manager _____ | PHOTO | Assistant _____ |

Manufacturing

| PHOTO | Manager _____ | PHOTO | Assistant _____ |

Etc, for finance, administration, purchasing

4.22 **Plan for quick weekly team briefing**

It is suggested that something like this be held every week to keep people aware of what's happening in the business. It should be held in a place where many people can gather and with most standing up – that should keep it short!

Suggested Topics	Brief Comments
New employees	
Employees who have left	
New contracts etc won	
Important customers lost	
New equipment that has arrived	
Developments in the world that might affect this business	
Requests for action by everyone. (Perhaps something like "Please be sure to put your papers away and turn off your computer at the end of the day.")	
Has anyone learned anything recently that might be shared with the rest of the people who work here?	
Any questions?	

_____

Briefing chaired by

_____

Date

It's not a bad idea to hand out this document and when complete, leave on the desks of those who were unable to attend.

4.23 **Employee benefits that a business might provide**

The main benefit to be aware of is (the now legal requirement) to provide pensions for your staff, which we go into in more detail elsewhere in this book.

Additional benefits might be:

- Death in Service
- Permanent Health Insurance

The above two (three if you include pensions) do not result in the employee having to pay tax on the premiums paid each year. However the items on the rest of this list attract both an income tax charge for the employee each year and the employer having to pay National Insurance (Class 1a) on the total benefit paid. Any contributions paid by the employee reduce the tax they have to pay.

- Private Medical Insurance.
- Cars, property, goods or other assets the ownership of which is transferred by the employer to the employee.
- Payments made by the employer on behalf of the employee.
- Vouchers given to the employee.
- Living accommodation
- Mileage allowance and passenger payments. If the mileage is incurred while travelling to visit a customer etc, and calculated in accordance with the rules (see www.hmrc.gov.uk/RATES/index.htm) that will not be liable to tax or National Insurance.
- Cars made available to the employee.
- Vans made available to the employee.
- Interest-free and low interest loans.
- Certain relocation expenses.
- Services supplied to the employee.
- Expense payments made to or on behalf of the employee such as:
- Entertainment
- Travelling and subsistence unless on employer business.
- General expense allowance.
- Payment for use of home telephone.

If you want information about the above list please go to the HMRC website and search for P11D Guide.

4.24 **Suggested self-employed contract form**

This form should be adapted for the particular circumstances prevailing and it should only be used if the underlying facts fit. It is unlikely to be valid if the conditions it contains are not adhered to.

SELF-EMPLOYED CONTRACT

THIS AGREEMENT is made the _____

day of _____

BETWEEN _____

of _____(hereinafter called 'the principal')

on the one part and _____

of _____(hereinafter called 'the contractor')

on the other part.

TERMS

1. The principle has agreed to supply the following services:

    a. _____

    b. _____

    c. _____

2. The dates between which the above services are to be supplied.

_____

3. Self-employment

The contractor shall supply his services to the principal as an independent contractor and nothing contained in this agreement or observed in the manner of its implementation shall create or be construed as implying or creating a relationship of master and servant or employer and employee between the principal and the contractor.

4. Payment

The Contractor shall submit invoices for these services and any agreed expenses on the last working day of the month and if approval is given, the principal will settle the invoice within two weeks or by other arrangement.

5. Liberty to supply a replacement

The contractor shall not be bound hereunder or otherwise to render personal services to the principal but may at his absolute discretion engage or appoint another person or other persons to render the required services in his stead.

6. Liberty to work elsewhere

The contractor shall be at liberty to supply his services to other principals provided only that the performance of services for other principals does not conflict with nor harm the interests of this principal.

4.24 **Suggested self-employed contract form** (continued)

7. Times of work

Neither the principal not any of the principal's officers and employees or agents shall have or acquire any right of control over the contractor as to the times at which or the methods whereby he performs the services required of him but these shall be rendered at such times and in such manner as the contractor himself shall decide subject only to the services being rendered within the term set for their performance and to the standard of performance specified by the principal. The principle shall not pay the contractor for times when the contractor is on holiday or is suffering from sickness.

8. Progress payments

The principal shall make such progress payments to the contractor as are specifically agreed from time to time between the principal and the contractor, such payments will retain the character of payments on account and in advance of the amount to be invoiced to the principal by the contractor on completion of the performance of the required services and shall not acquire the character of wages, salary of other emoluments however regular or equal to each other in amount the said payments on account might be.

9. Provision of tools and equipment

The contractor shall supply such tools equipment materials and assistance as may be necessary to perform the services required of him and the principal shall neither have nor assume any responsibilities obligations or liabilities in connection therewith either as regards the contractor himself or as regards any third party or parties and the contractor shall indemnify the principal in respect of any claims arising in connection therewith including claims for loss, damages or personal injury.

10. Liability for tax payments

The contractor shall discharge all such liabilities for income tax, national insurance and other taxes and levies as may accrue to him in respect of payments made to him by the principal for services rendered in accordance with this agreement and shall indemnify the principal in respect of any and all such liabilities.

11. Relationship

The relationship between the contractor and the principal as evidenced and perpetuated by this agreement shall neither be nor be regarded as being a relationship which will give rise to any rights or responsibilities whatsoever under employment protection legislation or under the statutory sick pay scheme.

12. Responsibility, customer care credo, uniform and general appearance

The contractor, when working on the principal's premises shall observe and obey all the laws and regulations that affect the principal with regard to Health and Safety, including those concerning the ban on smoking in the work place. However the contractor is not bound by any customer care credo that the principle practices. Nor shall the contractor be obliged to wear a uniform that indicates that he or she is part and parcel of the principle's work force.

4.24 **Suggested self-employed contract form** (continued)

13. Faulty workmanship

The contractor shall be responsible for making good any faulty workmanship in his own time and at his own expense.

14. Termination

This agreement shall terminate upon either party giving written notice of such termination to the other or upon either party being found to be in breach of any of its terms.

Signed_____   Signed_____

                     (Principal)   (Contractor)

Date _____   Date _____

AS WITNESS the hands of the parties the day and year first before written

Name_____   _____

Occupation_____   _____

Address_____   _____

_____   _____

Date_____   _____

N.B. If there are two witnesses, the second witness should write on the lines on the right.

4.25 **How to assess someone for possible redundancy**

Name		Department
Job Title	**Start Date**	**Length of Service**
Criteria	**Comments**	**Score out of 10**
Performance		
Job knowledge		
Team work		
Skills		
Experience		
Aptitude		
Attendance		
Proficiency		
Disciplinary record		
Responsibility		
Other		
Overall Score		

4.26 **How to calculate holiday entitlement**

Working Pattern	Holiday Entitlement
Full-time (5-day week)	5.6 weeks (28 days)
Part-time (4-day week)	5.6 weeks (22.4 days)
Part-time (3-day week)	5.6 weeks (16.8 days)
6-day week	5.6 weeks (28 days is the maximum entitlement)
Compressed hours (say 36 hours in four days)	36 hours x 5.6 weeks = 201.6 hours per year
Annualised hours (say 1,600 hours at an average of 33.5 hours per week)	(33.5 hours x 5.6 weeks = 187.6 hours per year)
Bank Holidays	Can be included in the 5.6 weeks leave – check the employment contract

4.27 **Discrimination in the workplace**

Employers must be aware of the dangers arising from discrimination against any of their workers. They should be aware that discrimination at work means unfair treatment by an employer which is, in some way, related to a personal characteristic, such as the following 'protected characteristics':

- age
- disability
- gender identity
- marriage or civil partnership
- pregnancy or maternity leave
- race
- religion or belief
- sex
- sexual orientation

There are different types of discrimination:

- direct discrimination
- harassment
- indirect discrimination
- victimisation
- reasonable adjustments
- discrimination arising from disability

Direct discrimination

This occurs when an employer treats someone worse than other people because of one of the protected personal characteristics listed above; for example, if an employee is not selected for promotion because of their race, this is direct race discrimination.

Harassment

Harassment is a form of discrimination covering a broad-ranging area that, again, involves those protected characteristics. It can include verbal abuse, suggestive remarks and unwanted physical contact.

Indirect discrimination

Indirect discrimination occurs where a particular employee is disadvantaged by a policy or requirement which is not justifiable in terms of the work. The disadvantage must be linked to one of the protected characteristics; for example, while not intending this to be the case, if the employer only gives training to full-time workers, this is likely to fall foul of discrimination law because it would almost certainly be indirectly discriminate against women, who are more likely to be part-time workers than men.

Victimisation

An employee may also be discriminated against if, as an employer, you victimise a person because he or she has tried to complain or take action about discrimination.

4.27 **Discrimination in the workplace** (continued)

Reasonable adjustments

Employers have a duty to remove the barriers that employees face because of disability. Employees must be free to both do their job and apply for a job in the same way as someone who is not disabled. This is called the duty to make reasonable adjustments.

Discrimination arising from disability

If an employee is disabled, an employer could also be guilty of discrimination against the disabled person if that person is treated unfairly because of something arising from that person's disability rather than the disability itself.

Employees who have been discriminated against at work can make a complaint or raise a grievance, and negotiate to try the resolve the issue; or an employee can make a claim to an employment tribunal. There's a strict time limit for making a tribunal claim. This is usually three months minus one day from the date when the thing that is being complained about last happened. Employees must notify The Advisory and Conciliation and Arbitration Service (ACAS) of their tribunal claim. This is so that they get advice about what to do before the time limit is up.

Employees can get also help from an experienced adviser, for example, at a Citizens Advice Bureau.

Bullying

While on this general subject of how employers may find themselves liable for mistreating their staff through discrimination, it would be no bad thing briefly to cover the subject of Bullying, examples of which might be:

- An employee being constantly criticised, or having duties and responsibility taken away without good reason.
- An employer who shouts, or behaves aggressively or makes threats.
- An employee who is put down or made to feel like the butt of the jokes.
- An employee who is persistently picked on in front of others or in private.
- An employee being constantly ignored, victimised and excluded regularly.
- An employer who constantly mocks and verbally attacks members of staff.
- Someone in the workplace who spreads malicious rumours about members of staff.
- Someone who misuses power or their position to make someone feel uncomfortable or victimised.
- An employer who makes threats about job security without any basis or substance.
- An employer who blocks promotion or progress within the workplace.

Employers should protect their staff from being bullied at work. ACAS has useful guidance about workplace bullying and harassment on its website at www.acas.org.uk.

5.01 **How to approach a possible lender with a request for finance**

The following steps are recommended if finance is being sought from a third party for any new project or business expansion:

1. Assemble up-to-date financial information, including where appropriate:

    a) Accounts for the most recent year

    b) Management accounts for the current period comparing actual results with budget

    c) Profit forecasts for future years

    d) Cash flow forecasts

    e) Projected balance sheets.

    If the latest accounts are out of date, the potential lender is not going to be impressed (see TTC 5.09, 'Understanding accounts' for more on this).

2. Consult a market research professional for his views on any new product you are considering. These experts see so many products fail and their experience in this field will either confirm or contradict your views and perhaps save a lot of time and money. The potential lender will be very interested in the result of this research.

3. Arrange an informal meeting with the potential lender at an early stage. Sound him out and, if he shows interest, tell him that a detailed report will be prepared.

4. Consider alternative sources of finance, such as:

    a) Sale of unwanted assets

    b) Existing cash balances (business or private)

    c) Leasing, hire purchase, renting, etc.

5. Prepare a short report for a potential lender. All reports will differ in content but the basic format should be one that the lender or an investor finds easy to grasp. The following is a suggested layout:

    a) Amount of money required and how it will be used

        Give very brief details of purpose, to introduce the reader to your needs. Also mention here the security you have available.

    b) Brief business history.

    c) Products or services

        i) Existing (if any)

            Say when the business was established

            Give description (including standard publicity and handouts).

        ii) Proposed.

            Give here the full details of what you are proposing to do.

    d) Names of professional advisers

        Mention accountants/auditors, solicitors, bankers, stockbrokers, design and marketing consultants. Give their contact details as an attachment to the report and state which of them have been consulted in preparing the report.

5.01 How to approach a possible lender with a request for finance (continued)

e) Audited accounts (if relevant)

Attach accounts for at least the previous two years or a shorter period if the business is younger. If the latest accounts are not finalised, include figures subject to audit.

f) Information on current trading position (if relevant)

Attach:

i) Management accounts comparing actual and budget for both revenue and capital

ii) Cash flow compared to budget

iii) Comments on variation.

g) Forecasts

Show forecasts and projections for existing business for subsequent years with existing products and existing finances (see TTC 5.05, 'Cash flow forecast sheet').

h) Forecasts to show the impact of the new venture or business expansion

Demonstrate exactly when and how borrowings will be repaid.

i) Market research

Mention briefly findings and conclusion of report.

j) Competition

Briefly comment on competitors.

k) Major customers

Identify them and indicate level of interest in project, product or expansion as the case may be.

l) Major suppliers

Identify and mention reliability.

m) Production and distribution plans

Refer to separate report if relevant and changes that are to be made.

n) Contingencies

Build into forecasts any likely risks and how they have been allowed for (e.g. 'We hope the product will be launched in September, but we are allowing for a delay until December.').

5.02 **Sample full business plan**

The following is a suggested layout of an elementary business plan:

1. **Amount of money required and how it will be used**
   Give very brief details of purpose, to introduce the reader to your needs. Also mention here the security you have available.

2. **Products or services**
   a) Existing (if any)
      i) Say when the business was established
      ii) Give description (including standard publicity and handouts).
   b) Proposed
      iii) Give here the full details of what you are proposing to do.

3. **Names of professional advisers**
   Mention accountants/auditors, solicitors, bankers, stockbrokers, design and marketing consultants. Give their contact details as an attachment to the report and state which of them have been consulted in preparing the report.

4. **Audited accounts** (if relevant)
   Attach accounts for at least the previous two years or a shorter period if the business is younger. If the latest accounts are not finalised, include figures subject to audit.

5. **Information on current trading position** (if relevant)
   Attach:
   a) Management accounts comparing actual and budget for both revenue and capital
   b) Cash flow compared to budget
   c) Comments on variation.

6. **Forecasts**
   Show forecasts and projections for existing business for subsequent years with existing products and existing finances.

7. **Forecasts to show the impact of the new venture or business expansion**
   Demonstrate exactly when and how borrowings will be repaid.

8. **Market research**
   Mention briefly findings and conclusion of report.

9. **Competition**
   Briefly comment on competitors.

10. **Major customers**
    Identify them and indicate level of interest in project, product or expansion as the case may be.

11. **Major suppliers**
    Identify and mention reliability.

12. **Production and distribution plans**
    Refer to separate report if relevant and changes that are to be made.

13. **Contingencies**
    Build into forecasts any likely risks and how they have been allowed for (e.g. 'We hope the product will be launched in September, but we are allowing for a delay until December.').

5.03 **KPIs**

KPIs stands for Key Performance Indicators. These are the things you measure on a regular basis to see how well or badly your business is doing (that's their first use) and their second use is even more important – KPIs enable you to manage your business better.

So how do you recognise a KPI when you see one?

The first KPI one thinks of, although it's not that useful, is the annual profit and loss account. This shows you what your sales have been, what your direct costs have been, how much your overheads were and what profit or loss you made. So, while it's an account (in other words, it tells a story), it shows you four vital figures, as well as other detailed figures that are key to measuring the performance of your business.

But this set of KPIs isn't that useful because it is usually prepared some months after the end of your accounting year, so it can be historical. It's not much use in terms of giving you up-to-date information.

So let's look at some big, bold and better KPIs.

The first is the bank balance. You may have a sheet in which you list the daily, weekly or monthly bank balance, so that you can see how it's moving, thus keeping a close and regular watch on where it's headed.

Then there is the figure of sales. Again, this could be daily, weekly, monthly and indeed it could (and should) be broken down between the different types of sales that you make.

Then there is the number of customers you have. You list the new ones that arrive and spot those that leave you. (In spite of your best efforts, you will find that this second figure is depressingly higher than you think it is. Customers die, move away, no longer have a need of your product or service. Just because they were customers last week, this is no guarantee that someone else won't wow them more than you have and that they will be won over to a rival tomorrow.)

Below I list a whole range of KPIs for you to consider using. You won't need too many, but you will want to have the right ones.

Some KPIs in regular use

To make this work, you should develop a simple template (a blank sheet of paper, even), on which to record the statistics that drive your business. It can even be handwritten – whatever you find suits you best. The key is to keep the template and use it to manage your business better.

Other KPIs, yields, ratios, etc.
- Sales in money
- Sales in numbers of sales
- Average sale
- Customer complaints
- Price of goods sold
- New products launched
- New guarantees launched
- New customers
- Customers lost
- New customer accounts opened
- Customer survey results
- Advertising costs
- Stocks held

Employee and productivity related
- Sales per employee
- Number of years' service of your employees
- Employee satisfaction survey results
- Absentee rate
- Hours of training by employees
- Costs of training and professional advancement

Other KPIs, yields, ratios, etc.
- Cash balances
- Gross margin

- Money owed by your business
- Money owed to your business
- Net profit percentage
- Dividends paid

And for the more technically minded
- Working capital
- Creditor and debtor turnover ratios

5.04 **Holding a mini business planning session**

In this sample agenda, I am going to deal with the 18 Great Leverage Points. (These were taught to me by my good friend Paul Dunn, who used to run Results Accountants Network.)

In my experience, using this agenda has never failed to produce a successful meeting.

Mini-Planning Session

Agenda for meeting at _____

1. **There are just four ways to grow a business**

    We can:

    a) increase the number of customers;

    b) increase the number of times they do business with us;

    c) increase the average value;

    d) increase our own effectiveness.

    What can we do to achieve improvements in this area?

2. **What you can measure you can manage**

    Here we need ideas for identifying whether our business is growing. The first is obviously the number of customers, but can anybody think of any other ways in which we can measure whether the business is going forward?

3. **The true purpose of any advertisement is to get a response**

    a) How effective is our advertising?

    b) Is there any other advertising we could do?

4. **Build in unique core differentiators, focus on them and articulate them constantly**

    What is it that our business does really well? In particular, is there something that other, similar businesses don't do (because that is the bit we want to get across)?

5. **Look for a second dimension**

    Do we know any other businesses that we could link up with?

6. **Learn to really listen**

    Are we asking our customers enough?

    Let's organise a customer survey or advisory board to ask our customers the following:

    a) What they think of us

    b) What we are doing right

    c) What we are doing wrong

    d) What we ought to be doing.

5.04 **Holding a mini business planning session** (continued)

7. **Cutting the price is always an easy option but there is usually a better way**

   We should think of increasing the value that we give rather than reducing the price.

8. **Lowering the barriers to doing business**

   Here we need to consider what it is that might prevent non-customers from crossing our threshold.

9. **The more you tell the more you sell**

   Are we telling our customers enough about our business?

10. **Avoid changing horses in midstream**

    The idea here is that after the meeting we should start a plan that we stick to for at least three months, preferably much longer. In other words, it's important for everybody sitting around the table to own the idea so that we really run with it confidently for a long enough period to see if it does work.

11. **What's in it for me (WIIFM)?**

    We know that our business is extremely good at caring for its customers. Therefore, in any advertisement, menu, newsletter, etc. we must identify the WIIFM factor and work on it.

12. **Learn the key frustrations**

    Most businesses are guilty of driving their customers mad. In the case of our business, it might be not serving the customers quickly enough. Only a customer advisory board will really find out what the frustrations are, but I am sure we can offer ideas under this heading. The idea is that we identify what all the other businesses in our industry get wrong and then eliminate them.

13. **Systematise**

    A really effective business is one that operates in a systematic way. Preferably, there should be written procedures so that every time we look after a client, he gets the same treatment.

    How standardised are our procedures? Is there a way in which they could be systematised better?

14. **Empowering our team**

    This is a very important subject and means recognising the ability that exists among our team members, giving them full responsibility and watching them develop, grow and enjoy working for us even more.

15. **Don't reverse the risk; remove it**

    What are the risks that our customers run when they do business with us and can we address them?

    What sort of guarantees can we give?

5.04 **Holding a mini business planning session** (continued)

16. **Give people a clear and detailed action plan**

    This will develop from the need for the proprietors to have developed a long-term goal. This goal needs to be declared and owned by everybody. Once that happens, we build a long-term action plan, using Key Performance Indicators to see how well we are going along the path, then everybody can use this as a map to see how successful the business is.

17. **Create offers to add value and to encourage quicker responses**

    Are there any offers that we could make?

18. **Adding the third dimension**

    The basic question here is, 'Which other companies have the customers that we are trying to reach?'

    The crux of the matter is that our potential clients are already customers of other businesses. If we can think of firms that have those customers, could we develop joint ventures with those companies to gain access to those clients?

WHAT AN ACTION PLAN LOOKS LIKE

There are two types of action plan, but they both aim at one result – action/results.

The first, and more important, plan concerns those things that you are going to start doing now (the list of top priorities). The second is the list of those things that you will do one day. (They may not be urgent but you don't want to lose sight of them.) So the top priorities have to be attended to first.

Now, please feel free to tweak this – for it to work you have to be happy with the plan itself, but, in principle, I believe the first action plan should look like this:

List of top priorities	Action (description)	By whom (who is responsible for achieving these points?)	By when

5.04 **Holding a mini business planning session** (continued)

The list of second priorities would be similar:

Action (description)	Initial responsibility lies with	Possible date for completion

And then, once you have achieved an action, it's very important to have a list of points that have been dealt with so that everyone can see that the whole process is really achieving things of value. It will add momentum to the process.

List of actions completed

Action (description)	Date completed	By whom

5.05 **Cash flow forecast sheet**

Your business name	CASH FLOW FORECAST – PERIOD:				
	Initial	1	2	3	4
Month:	balance	**Apr**	**May**	**June**	**July**
Receipts					
Cash sales					
Credit sales					
VAT reclaimed					
Bank loans/loans received					
Capital introduced					
Other					
Total receipts					
Expenditure					
Cost of sales (purchases)					
Subcontractor					
Other direct costs					
Employee costs					
Premises costs					
Repairs					
General administrative expenses					
Motoring					
Travel and subsistence					
Advertising and promotion					
Entertainment					
Legal and professional					
Bank interest					
Other finance charges					
Other expenses					
Cash drawn from bank					
Personal drawings					
Capital purchases					
Loan repayments					
Transfers					
VAT					
Total expenditure					
Cash flow surplus/Deficit (–)					
Opening bank balance					
Closing bank balance					

5.05 **Cash flow forecast sheet** (continued)

5	6	7	8	9	10	11	12	
Aug	Sept	Oct	Nov	Dec	Jan	Feb	Mar	Total

5.06 **Budget sheet**

Income and Expenditure Budget   Accounting year ending _____

EXPECTED SALES   _____ A

less

- **Cost of sales** e.g. raw materials and stocks   _____
  Construction industry subcontractors costs   _____
  Other direct costs e.g. packing and despatch   _____
  Total cost of sales   _____ B
  Gross profit or loss A – B   _____ C
  Other income   _____ D

EXPECTED EXPENDITURE

- **Employee costs** – Salaries, wages, bonuses, employer's NIC, pension contributions, casual wages, canteen costs, recruitment agency fees, subcontractors (unless shown above) and other wages costs   _____
- **Premises costs** – Rent, ground rent, rates, water, refuse, light and heat, property insurance, security and use of home   _____
- **Repairs** – Repair of property, replacements, renewals, maintenance   _____
- **Telephone, postage and communication costs** – Telephone, fax, mobile telephone, stationery, photocopying, printing, postage, courier, computer costs, subscriptions and insurance   _____
- **Motoring expenses and travel** – Petrol, servicing, licence, repairs, motor insurance, hire and leasing, car parking, RAC/AA membership   _____
- **Travel and subsistence** – Rail, air, bus, etc. travel, taxis, subsistence and hotel costs   _____
- **Entertainment** – Staff entertaining (e.g. Christmas party), customer gifts up to £10 per person advertising your business   _____
- **Advertising and promotion** – Advertising, promotion, mailshots, free samples, brochures, newsletters, trade shows, etc.   _____
- **Legal and professional costs** – Accountancy, legal, architects, surveyors, stocktakers' fees, indemnity insurance   _____
- **Bad debts**
  (see HMRC notes for guidance)   _____
- **Interest** – Bank loans, overdraft, other loans   _____
- **Other finance charges** – Bank charges, HP interest, credit card charges, leasing not already included   _____
- **Depreciation and losses on sale**
  (see HMRC notes for guidance)   _____
- **Other items**   _____

Grand total of expenditure   _____ E
Expected net profit (or loss)   C + D – E   _____

5.07 **Income and expenditure account**

Income and Expenditure Account — Accounting year ending _____

SALES INCOME _____ A

less

- **Cost of sales** e.g. raw materials and stocks _____
- **Construction industry subcontractors costs** _____
- **Other direct costs** e.g. packing and despatch _____
- **Total cost of sales** _____ B
- **Gross profit or loss A – B** _____ C
- **Other income** _____ D

EXPECTED EXPENDITURE

- **Employee costs** – Salaries, wages, bonuses, employer's NIC, pension contributions, casual wages, canteen costs, recruitment agency fees, subcontractors (unless shown above) and other wages costs _____
- **Premises costs** – Rent, ground rent, rates, water, refuse, light and heat, property insurance, security and use of home _____
- **Repairs** – Repair of property, replacements, renewals, maintenance _____
- **Telephone, postage and communication costs** – Telephone, fax, mobile telephone, stationery, photocopying, printing, postage, courier, computer costs, subscriptions and insurance _____
- **Motoring expenses and travel** – Petrol, servicing, licence, repairs, motor insurance, hire and leasing, car parking, RAC/AA membership _____
- **Travel and subsistence** – Rail, air, bus, etc. travel, taxis, subsistence and hotel costs _____
- **Entertainment** – Staff entertaining (e.g. Christmas party), customer gifts up to £10 per person advertising your business _____
- **Advertising and promotion** – Advertising, promotion, mailshots, free samples, brochures, newsletters, trade shows, etc. _____
- **Legal and professional costs** – Accountancy, legal, architects, surveyors, stocktakers fees, indemnity insurance _____
- **Bad debts** (see HMRC notes for guidance) _____
- **Interest** – Bank loans, overdraft, other loans _____
- **Other finance charges** – Bank charges, HP interest, credit card charges, leasing not already included _____
- **Depreciation and losses on sale** (see HMRC notes for guidance) _____
- **Other items** _____

Grand total of expenditure _____ E

Net profit (or loss) C + D – E _____

5.08 **Layout of VAT invoice**

Design an appropriate VAT invoice, based on the simple example shown below, if any of your sales are to be made to credit customers, i.e. not for cash at point of sale.

Date   01.11.15   VAT Invoice No 001

A. Trader

22 North Road, Tavistock PL19 9NC
Telephone: (01822) 12345 Fax: (01822) 54321 Email: atrader@uk
VAT Registration No 123 4567 89

To   A. Customer
                   10 Oakdale Road, Tavistock PL10 2NP

Quantity	Description	Cost £	p	VAT %	£	p
1,000	Torches @ £15	15,000	00	20	3,000	00
2	Radios @ £120	240	00	20	48	00
1	Battery		25	20		05
Total Sales		£ 15,240 :	25		3,048 :	05
Add Total VAT		£ 3,048 :	05			
Net Total of Invoice		£ 18,288 :	30			

5.09 **Understanding accounts**

Accountants' clients may not be able, or willing, to understand financial statements. But here's a quick outline to help you to do so.

Why prepare accounts?

1. Unless you are in business for enjoyment alone, you are necessarily in business to make a profit. Having established this point it becomes obvious that you will want to find out how much profit or loss your business is making. This is exactly what a profit and loss account demonstrates and is probably the most important figure contained in the accounts. However, you will find other important information as well.

2. Accounts have to be prepared by law.

3. Accounts have to be prepared for the taxman.

    Numbers 2 and 3 are negative reasons for preparing accounts (i.e. you only prepare accounts because you are compelled), so let us concentrate on the positive reason – namely that the documents are informative.

The profit and loss account

Essentially this is a comparatively easy statement to understand. It lists the money that a business has received (or is due to receive) during the period covered by the accounts and, from them, deducts the money the business has paid out (or has been due to pay out) during the period (expenditure). The difference is the profit or loss.

If the statement is read slowly and carefully, there should be no problem in understanding it, especially if you remember exactly why it has been prepared – to show you how well or badly the business has done during the period covered by the accounts.

There are, however, two accounting expressions which may be a little difficult to understand. These are:

1. **Stocks:** In most businesses there are goods bought in one accounting period and sold in another. The cost of these goods should be charged, not against the profits of the period in which they were bought but against the profits of the period in which they were sold. It's necessary to deduct the cost of any unsold stocks at the end of the period covered by the accounts, as this cost will be added to the relevant future accounting period.

    Such stocks are called 'closing stocks' and, if the accounts contain a figure of 'opening stocks', you will realise that this figure refers to unsold stocks at the end of the previous accounting period.

2. **Depreciation:** In a business you own plant machinery and/or equipment which will wear out in time. Depreciation is the accountant's estimate of how much this property of the business has worn out during the period covered by the accounts.

The balance sheet

As explained, the profit and loss account shows how much the business has made or lost during the period covered by the accounts. It's an 'account' or 'story'. The balance sheet shows how much, in theory, the business was worth at the end of the period covered by the accounts. It's a 'photograph' of the business at a particular date.

The balance sheet is divided into two parts – part 1, the statement of total net assets, shows the net total value of everything the business owns less everything it owes – in theory, how much the business is worth.

Part 2, the statement of source of finance, shows how the assets listed in part 1 have been paid for.

5.09 **Understanding accounts** (continued)

Total net assets

As with the profit and loss account, read it through slowly and carefully bearing in mind the purpose of the statement. Here, again, there are certain accounting terms which may need further explanation:

- **Assets:** The word asset is an omnibus term for anything the business owns.
- **Fixed assets:** A fixed asset is something bought for the business for use in running the business (e.g. a factory or machine).
- **Current assets:** A current asset is something paid for, which is intended to turn into profit within the near future (e.g. stocks).
- **Depreciation:** Depreciation is the amount by which the accountant has estimated the asset has worn out since it was first bought.
- **Stocks:** These are bought with the intention of reselling them in one form or another at a later date. Thus any unsold stocks at an accounting period end form part of the current assets at that date.
- **Debtors:** This is the money owed to a business by its customers, etc.
- **Prepayments:** These are usually payments made in advance. For example, an insurance premium may have been paid up to a date after the balance sheet date. The amount paid in advance is, theoretically, repayable by the insurance company and, as such, is like a debtor, but is called a prepayment.
- **Current liabilities:** This refers to money which a business owes to other people.
- **Creditors:** This is the most usual type of current liability and therefore refers to money owed by the business as at the balance sheet date.
- **Working capital:** This is the total of current assets less current liabilities. It's a net total thrown up within the balance sheet and, in crude terms, if fixed assets form the engine which runs the business, working capital is the fuel of that engine.

The source of finance

I've established that part 1 of the balance sheet shows you how much a business is worth in theory. However, to round off the statement it must be shown how the net assets have been paid for (i.e. how they have been financed). The usual sources of finance are:

Proprietor's funds

- **Capital introduced:** This is the money that the owner of the business has 'put up' to start the business as well as any additional funds he may have contributed.
- **Profits:** If the business has been making profits, the money thereby created will have paid for some of the assets. Profits are a source of finance.
- **Losses:** If the business has been making losses, then money will have flowed out of the business – hence losses are a deduction from proprietor's funds.

  (As any profit or loss, as shown in the balance sheet, will have come from the profit and loss account, the two figures on the statements should be the same.)
- **Drawings:** This is the money you have drawn from the business to live off.

Loans to the business

If a bank or anyone else has lent money to the business, it is another source of finance.

5.10 **What an accountant needs to prepare your accounts**

The most important thing to remember is to keep some sort of record for every single transaction – whether it be income or expenditure. If no record is kept, how will you remember, or your accountant even know, that the transaction took place?

Some people fail on purpose to keep a proper and complete record of their income, hoping thereby to save tax. This sort of behaviour is wrong, dishonest and illegal. On top of this lies the fact that HMRC nearly always find out that this has been going on and in revenge (as it were) collect all the unpaid tax going back for as many years as necessary. They will also charge interest on the late payment and penalties (i.e. fines) as well, by way of punishment. Thus it is both wrong and not worth it to fail to keep proper and complete records. This said, we can move on to the records.

An accountant needs the following in order to prepare accounts and the law also requires you to keep:

- Cheque book counterfoils
- Invoices for expenses paid by cheque
- Invoices for expenses paid in cash
- Paying-in books
- Copy sales invoices or other vouchers giving evidence to all monies received by cheque and cash
- Bank statements
- Wages records
- Any other books in which you have recorded your transactions, for example the analysis of cash and cheques, etc. paid out document (see TTC 5.11).

At the end of the accounting period he will also need:

- A statement of money owed by you – creditors
- A statement of money owed to you – debtors
- A list of unsold stocks on hand at the end of your accounting period.

Hence, as long as you have methodically kept all the above items, the accountant should have got sufficient information to prepare accurate accounts.

Remember also to keep your business records for six years.

5.11 Sheet showing analysis of cash and cheques, etc. paid out

Date	Name and Description (where necessary)	Cheque Number	Total Cash Payments	Total Cheque Payment	Input VAT	Cost of Sales (Purchases)	Sub-Contractor	Other Direct Costs (Packaging etc)				Employee Costs	Premises Costs	Repairs	General Administrative Expenses
1.9.15	A.B.Smith	1		540 50	90 08	450 42									
1.9.15	C.D.Jones	2		587 50	97 92	489 58									
2.9.15	Post Offices Counters		15 00												15 00
2.9.15	E.F.Brown	3		115 00	19 17										
3.9.15	Cash	4		100 00											
3.9.15	Wages	5		350 00								350 00			
4.9.15	HMRC	6		100 00								100 00			
4.9.15	E.F.Brown		30 00												
5.9.15	M.N.Stores		13 00												13 00
5.9.15	E.F.Brown	7		5,000 00											
5.9.15	Cash	8		50 00											
5.9.15	A.B.Smith	9		180 00											
5.9.15	Telecom	10		127 00	21 17										
6.9.15	O.P.Sanderson		98 00		16 33										
6.9.15	G.H.Landlord	11		350 00									350 00		
7.9.15	I.J.Insurance	12		150 00											150 00
7.9.15	K.L.Green	13		125 00	20 83										104 17
7.9.15	Connex South Central	14		20 00											
			156 00	7,795 00	265 50	940 00						450 00	350 00		282 17
				£7,951.00											
						940 00							350 00		282 17

V = Votable Inputs
(V) = Possible VAT Inputs

Enter total Inputs excluding VAT in this box = £6,904.00

5.11 Sheet showing analysis of cash and cheques, etc. paid out (continued)

Motoring	Travel & Subsistence	Advertising & Promotion	Entertainment	Legal & Professional	Bank Interest	Other Finance Charges		Other Expense	Detail	Cash Drawn from Bank	Personal Drawings	Capital Purchases	Loan Repayments	Transfers	Sales					
							1													
							2													
							3													
95 83							4													
							5			100 00										
							6													
							7													
30 00							8													
							9													
							10					5,000 00	New Car							
							11				50 00									
							12				180 00									
105 83							13													
							14								81 67					
							15													
							16													
							17													
	20 00						18													
							19													
231 66	20 00						20			100 00	230 00	5,000 00			81 67					
							21													
							22													
							23													
							24													
							25													
							26													
							27													
							28													
							29													
							30													
231 66	20 00											5,000 00			81 67					
V	V	V	(V)	V				(V)		V			(V)	(V)	(V)	(V)				

5.12 **The six steps to financial control**

1. Establish your anticipated income from sales (including VAT) for the year.

2. Establish your cost of sales, i.e. purchase of goods for processing or resale (including VAT) for the year.

3. Establish your overheads and outgoings, etc. (do not forget VAT payments, loan repayments, capital purchases, contingencies, taxation and drawings, all including VAT) for the year.

4. Ensure that 1 is greater than 2 + 3.

5. Divide the total of 2 + 3 by 12. This is the maximum you may spend in any month. Never exceed it. Any bills that would push you over this limit must wait until the next month to be paid.

6. Divide your total sales by 12 and ensure that your sales invoices total at least reaches this figure each month; then work on your customers to keep the cash coming in.

Result: The finances will look after themselves.

5.13 **What expenses can I claim against tax?**

There is a general rule that any business expenses must be incurred wholly and exclusively for the purposes of the business. This means that some expenses will fall foul of the so-called dual purpose rule. For example, if you attend a business conference in Spain and tack a holiday on the end, your trip will have a dual purpose and the expenses won't be allowed. However, according to HMRC, 'in practice some dual purpose expenses include an obvious part which is for the purposes of the business. We usually allow the deduction of a proportion of expenses like that', and they go on to give the example of car or van expenses.

BASIC COSTS AND GENERAL RUNNING EXPENSES

✔ **Normally allowed** – The cost of goods bought for resale and raw materials used in business. Advertising, delivery charges, heating, lighting, cleaning, rates, telephone. The rent of business premises. The replacement of small tools and special clothing. Postage, stationery, relevant books and magazines. Accountants' fees. Bank charges on business accounts. Fees to professional bodies. Security expenditure.

✘ **Not allowed** – The initial cost of machinery, vehicles, equipment – but you can claim capital allowances on so-called 'integral features'. The cost of buildings. Providing for anticipated expenses in the future.

USE OF HOME FOR WORK

✔ **Normally allowed** – The business proportion of telephone calls and line rental, lighting, heating, cleaning, insurance, rent, Council Tax and mortgage interest. Provided you don't use any part of your home exclusively for business purposes, you won't lose your entitlement to private residence relief for Capital Gains Tax.

WAGES AND SALARIES

✔ **Normally allowed** – Wages, salaries, redundancy and leaving payments paid to employees. Pensions for past employees and their dependants. Staff training.

✘ **Not allowed** – Your own wages or salary or that of any business partner. Your own drawings.

TAX AND NATIONAL INSURANCE

✔ **Normally allowed** – Employer's National Insurance Contributions for employees. Reasonable pay for your spouse, provided he or she is actually employed.

✘ **Not allowed** – Income Tax. Capital Gains Tax. Inheritance Tax. Your own National Insurance Contributions.

ENTERTAINING

✔ **Normally allowed** – Entertainment of own staff (e.g. a Christmas party).

✘ **Not allowed** – Any other business entertaining.

PRE-TRADING

✔ **Normally allowed** – Revenue business expenditure incurred within seven years before starting to trade.

5.13 **What expenses can I claim against tax?** (continued)

GIFTS

✔ **Normally allowed** – Gifts costing up to £50 a year to each person so long as the gift advertises your business (or things it sells). Gifts (whatever their value) to employees.

✘ **Not allowed** – Food, drink, tobacco or vouchers for goods given to anyone other than employees.

TRAVELLING

✔ **Normally allowed** – Hotel and travelling expenses on business trips. Travel between different places of work. The running costs of your own car - whole of cost if used wholly for business, proportion if used privately too.

✘ **Not allowed** – Travel between home and business. The cost of buying a car or van (but you can claim capital allowances).

Leased cars with CO_2 emissions of more than 160g/km will have 15 per cent of the leasing payments disallowed. There is no restriction for cars with CO_2 emissions of less than or equal to 160g/km.

INTEREST PAYMENTS

✔ **Normally allowed** – The interest on overdrafts and loans for business purposes.

✘ **Not allowed** – The interest on capital paid or credited to partners.

HIRE PURCHASE

✔ **Normally allowed** – Interest element of instalments (i.e. not the capital cost).

✘ **Not allowed** – Capital element of instalments (but you may get capital allowances).

HIRING

✔ **Normally allowed** – Reasonable charge for hire of capital goods, including cars.

INSURANCE

✔ **Normally allowed** – Business insurance (e.g. employer's liability, fire and theft, motor, insuring employees' lives).

✘ **Not allowed** – Your own life insurance.

TRADEMARKS

✔ **Normally allowed** – Fees paid to register a trademark, design or patent.

✘ **Not allowed** – The cost of buying a patent from someone else (but you may get capital allowances).

LEGAL COSTS

✔ **Normally allowed** – The costs of recovering debts, defending business rights, preparing service agreements, appealing against rates, renewing a lease for a period not exceeding 50 years (but not if a premium is paid).

✘ **Not allowed** – Expenses (including Stamp Duty) for acquiring land, buildings or leases. Fines and other penalties for breaking the law, for example parking/speeding fines.

5.13 **What expenses can I claim against tax?** (continued)

REPAIRS
✔ **Normally allowed** – Normal repairs and maintenance to premises or equipment.
✘ **Not allowed** – The cost of additions, alterations, improvements (but you may get capital allowances).

DEBTS
✔ **Normally allowed** – Specific provisions for debts and debts written off.
✘ **Not allowed** – General reserve for bad or doubtful debts.

SUBSCRIPTIONS
✔ **Normally allowed** – Payments which secure benefits for your business or staff. Payments to societies that have arrangements with HMRC (in some cases only a proportion).
✘ **Not allowed** – Payments to political parties, churches and charities (but small gifts to local churches and charities may be allowed).

Travelling and subsistence expenses and tax

Expenses	Employer	Self-employed	Can VAT (Input Tax) be reclaimed?
	Where expenses are incurred by the employer, whether a self-employed trader, a partnership or a company	Where a self-employed trader incurs these expenses on his own behalf	
Entertaining own staff	Allowable	Allowable	Yes*
Business travel between place of business and customers, etc. (but not home)	Allowable	Allowable	Yes
Hotel bills, etc.	Allowable	Allowable	Yes, so long as it's billed to the VAT-registered trader
Drinks and meals away from home:			
1. Working/selling	Allowable	Not allowable	Yes*
2. On training course	Allowable	Allowable	Yes*

5.13 **What expenses can I claim against tax?** (continued)

Expenses	Employer	Self-employed	Can VAT (Input Tax) be reclaimed?
3. Buying, trips, etc.	Allowable	Allowable	Yes*
Entertaining business clients	Not allowable	Not allowable	No
Car parking	Allowable	Allowable	Yes
Trade show expenses	Allowable	Allowable	Yes
Fuel	Allowable	Allowable (business proportion only)	Yes**

* But not if there is any measurable degree of business entertainment.

** But if the Input VAT is reclaimed, remember to include the scale charge in your Output tax on the VAT Return.

6.01 **Suggested business continuity plan**

Imagine you went to work one day and discovered that you couldn't get to your building because an unexploded bomb had been found near your place of work. And then while you were waiting, wondering what to do next, the bomb went up, destroying all your business.

How would you cope? How would you get your business back? How would you pay your people? How would you answer the phones? How would you tell your customers what had happened and what you were doing to return to normal service as soon as possible?

It's a daunting thought and one hopes it will never happen. And yet, and yet … I have seen exactly this happen to a business near my home. A man driving a car, with which he was unfamiliar, drove into a pedestrian on a pavement and crushed him against the shop front of our local estate agents. The pedestrian was rushed to hospital by air ambulance, the police and fire brigade were very much in evidence, as was the 'Do not Cross tape', and shops were disrupted. The car park was closed and there was a scene of general chaos.

The estate agents premises were so badly damaged that, as I type this, over one month later, those premises are still closed – business is no longer being done there.

Could it happen to you?

Well, we hope not; but these things evidently do happen and it is as well to develop a plan for dealing with such an event.

Any such plan should be laid out as follows – as you will see, it is divided into three sections:

1. **Immediate actions** – to try to help the people who may need hospitalisation
2. **Recovery actions** – to try to get the business going again as soon as possible at an alternative location
3. **Return to normal actions** – to try to re-establish the business as if nothing had happened.

1. **Immediate action plan:**
    a) Create a Small Emergency Response Team, who will …
    b) Attend to anyone who has injuries.
    c) Call emergency services if they are not already at the scene.
    d) Assess if any employees or visitors to the business are not accounted for.
    e) Instruct all members of staff who may still be unaware of the crisis.
    f) Inform the insurance company.

2. **Recovery actions:**
    a) Create a small Crisis Management Team, who will …
    b) Assess what, if anything, is still usable in the office:
        i) Computers
        ii) Phones
        iii) Electricity, gas and water
        iv) Furniture.

6.01 **Suggested business continuity plan** (continued)

    c)   If temporary alternative premises are required:

        i)   Find some.

        ii)   Find the latest computer back-up tape.

        iii)   Order or hire replacement furniture.

3.   **Return to normality plan** – this will be for the business to devise at their leisure but we provide some thoughts in the table below.

Business Continuity Plan

Business name.	
IMMEDIATE ACTION PLAN	
Members of Emergency Response Team	**Phone numbers, etc. and action points**
1.	
2.	
3.	
Emergency services	
Have they been phoned?	☐ Yes ☐ No
Insurance company	
Have they been phoned?	☐ Yes ☐ No
Names of employees	
1.	
2.	
3.	
4.	
5.	
Etc.	
Have they been phoned?	☐ Yes ☐ No
RECOVERY ACTION PLAN	
Crisis Management Team	**Phone numbers, etc. and action points**
1.	
2.	
3.	
Create a plan for resuming normal business service	Done? ☐ Yes ☐ No
Find alternative premises	Done? ☐ Yes ☐ No

6.01 **Suggested business continuity plan** (continued)

Find alternative furniture	Done? ☐ Yes ☐ No
Find alternative computers	Done? ☐ Yes ☐ No
Name of landlords	
Have they been phoned?	☐ Yes ☐ No
Local estate agent for rentable office space	
Have they been phoned?	☐ Yes ☐ No
Who has the computer back-up tapes?	
Have they been phoned?	☐ Yes ☐ No
Computer supplier	
Have they been phoned?	☐ Yes ☐ No
Phone company	
Have they been phoned?	☐ Yes ☐ No
Software suppliers	
Have they been phoned?	☐ Yes ☐ No
Electricity supplier	
Have they been phoned?	☐ Yes ☐ No
Gas supplier	
Have they been phoned?	☐ Yes ☐ No
Water company	
Have they been phoned?	☐ Yes ☐ No
Furniture supplier	
Have they been phoned?	☐ Yes ☐ No
Normal maintenance/repair engineer	
Have they been phoned?	☐ Yes ☐ No
Electrician	
Have they been phoned?	☐ Yes ☐ No
Bank	
Have they been phoned?	☐ Yes ☐ No
Who has a copy of the database of names of customers?	
Which customers need prompt notification	
1.	
2.	
3.	
Etc.	

6.01 **Suggested business continuity plan** (continued)

Have they been phoned?	Done? ☐ Yes ☐ No
Consider how wages will be paid	Done? ☐ Yes ☐ No
Where are the originals of all the company's key documents such as leases, employment contracts, car registration insurance and MOT documents?	
Who will deal with the Press – if they want a comment?	

RETURN TO NORMAL ACTION PLAN	
Return to Normal Management Team	**Phone numbers, etc. and action points**
1.	
2.	
3..	
Assess the financial impact of this crisis	Done? ☐ Yes ☐ No
Decide whether to return to old premises or find new	Done? ☐ Yes ☐ No
Contact bank explaining needs	Done? ☐ Yes ☐ No
Contact customers telling them what will happen	Done? ☐ Yes ☐ No
Make plans to move to permanent accommodation	Done? ☐ Yes ☐ No

6.02 **Schedule of equipment for insurance purposes**

Class of item

(e.g. Factory plant, office equipment, office furniture, computers)

Item	Date of purchase	Supplier and address	Purchase cost	Model and number	Serial number	Insured value	Is that enough? ✔ if so

8.01 **The importance of delegation**

If you have systems that others can follow, use and help to run your business, then you must delegate this work to them.

To some people 'delegating' is a dirty word. It sounds like getting rid of the work you don't want to do: palming it off to some poor soul who cannot refuse to do it. I hope, by the time you have finished this short point, that you will see that proper delegating is a valuable tool in your business growth armoury.

The first point about delegating is that you have to do it. The saying goes that if you can free up your time by (probably) 80 per cent, you will have created a huge reservoir of time for you to plan and manage your business.

The second point is, and this may surprise you, that if you pass on some of your responsibilities to someone working with you, he is far more likely to get excited by the opportunity this affords him than being brassed off by having more work to do. Employees love to excel and, when it comes to giving them new jobs, work and responsibilities, they are likely to relish what you give them, rather than resent it.

If you give them the job to do, then give them the tools of the job as well. Give them free rein to do it and say, 'This system is the one I have been using. If you can think of a better one, let me know and, chances are, I'll give you the wherewithal to try out your ideas.'

So, having got this far, you will find that, in a short space of time, they could easily be doing the job better than you were. None of us can assume that our method is the best or the only method there is. After all, two heads are often better than one, and the very act of delegating could well spark a whole new method of working and an improvement to the bottom line.

With delegating comes the need to train and this means that time and money must be invested in making sure the person understands what it is that he should be doing. He may even need to go on a course or get an extra qualification. But by investing in your people, you will find that they reward you with better work, better systems, a happier workforce and better profits.

Not a bad deal, eh?

8.02 **Make sure your debtors pay up**

TELEPHONE THEM BEFORE IT'S TOO LATE

From time to time our clients say, 'I don't believe I've made £X profit because I've only got £Y in the bank'. The reply to this is usually that, if all debtors had paid, they would have got X + Y in the bank.

It is sometimes forgotten that money owed by debtors if often the repose of the profits that the business has made. If the debtors don't pay that money over, then the profits vanish.

In order to ensure that debtors do pay it is vital to plan the collection of the debts. Not only will this lead to the more prompt payment of your debts but it will also show your debtors that you mean business and are well organised. Such a plan will increase the respect that you have in the business world.

This plan consists of:

1. Keeping a close day-to-day control of your debtors. On the assumption that you allow 30 days for the payment you should mark out in advance the day on which each bill becomes overdue and be prepared to telephone your customer a few days later.

2. You should then plan the call for each customer whose account is outstanding. You should make a note of the date of the bill, its number, its amount and a rough description of what it is for. You should also have a record of the past payment record of this particular customer, and any subsequent sales to him, and you should be prepared, before the call, to admit and apologise if you have made any mistakes. You should also be prepared, before you telephone your customer, to suggest that the debt be settled by standing order to payments by instalments and if you decide to do this, you should have an exact figure of each instalment and the number of payments required.

3. You should then telephone your customer, having made a precise note of the correct telephone number and appropriate person to speak to, and first of all be polite. You should ask him how he is and how his business is. You might also point out that you like to contact your clients after you have supplied them with goods or services to make sure that they are satisfied and to show them you are interested in them. You then say that you notice that your account, which is due for payment by a certain date, is a few days overdue – please not that at this stage that it is only a few days overdue-and you ask if there are any problems in settling the amount. You then pause to let your customer feel the silence and realise that, while you have fulfilled your part of the deal, he has not fulfilled his. At the end of this pause he should come up with an appropriate, we hope positive, answer and, if he offers payments, you should agree with him that a cheque for £X will be sent to you within the next few days. Having established that the customer is going to do this you then conclude the call by saying that you will expect his cheque by a certain date and that you hope to do business with him again in the near future – or something of the sort.

4. You then follow up this call by making sure that the customer fulfils the agreement that you have made on the telephone call. If the cheque has not arrived by the date that he said it would, you then telephone him again. And you keep on telephoning him being as polite as you can until the cheque arrives.

The main point about collecting debts is not to have a row with the customer who is late in paying but to collect his money. If you have a row and threaten legal proceedings, it usually only delays payment and adds expense. If you are courteous to him, he is likely to be courteous to you and not only will you get the money from him but also you will probably get more business.

As with all business matters collecting debts is simply a matter of planning and good management. In the case of the few customers who are late in paying their bills if you follow the above rules you should find that there very few bad payers.

8.03 **How to set out a press release**

If you want to get something in the Press, you have simply got to make it easy for the Press to do as you wish. They will have a stack of stories to deal with and choose from and, if you want them to pick yours, you should lay the story out in a properly drawn-up Press Release (see below).

It's a good idea to phone the paper before submitting it to warn them that there is a release on its way and to ask for the appropriate email address of the addressee.

How to set out a Press Release

A Press Release should have the following general layout:

1. No more than one side of A4.

2. Photograph.

3. Concise caption.

4. Brief description of the story in one or two sentences.

5. More information over (say) five or six paragraphs.

6. Date and time for release.

7. Contact details, including mobile phones and emails.

8. An offer to call in and meet to discuss the story if required or offer to take the journalist out for a drink or a meal. Journalists are not well paid and appreciate being 'looked after'.

9. A promise to supply further information about subsequent developments.

10. It should be in email format for ease of use at the newspaper.

11. Make a follow-up phone call to see if it has arrived.

8.04 **Sample agenda for a meeting**

Agenda for [*office*] meeting at [*time*] on [*date*] in [*where*]

Who is invited to attend:_____

1. Apologies

2. Approval of minutes of previous meeting

3. Matters arising
    a) Website
    b) Invoice production
        Etc.

4. Financial report

5. Developments since last meeting

6. What we have learned on courses we have attended since the last meeting

7. Any other business to be referred to the chairman before the meeting

8. Date of next meeting.

At the end of the meeting the chairman will ask if the meeting has met everyone's expectations – to judge whether the meeting has been a success/worthwhile, etc.

8.05 **Sample minutes of business meeting**

Agenda for [*office*] meeting at [*time*] on [*date*] in [*where*]

Present: HMW (chairman), TJS, DJ, SC, AS, BH, IRW, MD, LS, SL, JB, RP

1. Apologies: KS, WK, AG **ACTION**

   Welcome. HMW welcomed the two new employees, SL and JB to their first office meeting.

2. Minutes of previous meeting were approved.

3. Matters arising

   a) Website. This is being redesigned. Comments were made that it now looks dated and does not include mention of everyone. We will also need to include SL and JB. AS volunteered to take over the website and get in touch with the designer. Issues such as how much more was the website costing, and could we find a similar typed alternative were discussed.   HMW AS

   b) Invoices. HMW suggested that although WK had done a very good job with designing the invoice he still had some reservations with the spacing and layout. It was suggested that WK (in her absence) and JB may like to look at the report design and contact XYZ to find out if it is possible to reduce the odd-looking gaps in the present design and any potential cost if we need their help. We can then decide whether this is the way we want to go.   JB WK

   c) Going paperless. HMW asked the question of everyone that, if we can extricate ourselves from ABC, would what we have currently (i.e. scanning via the Konica machine) be sufficient for us to go paperless without buying a specific product? SC and IRW pointed out that if we involve any other paperless businesses we should set out what we need them to do, rather than being told what the software can do and try to work around this.

4. Financial report

   a) The chief accountant announced that the rolling total of sales was still increasing but that there had been significant complaints about the recent increase in prices for those clients who were not economical to serve at their historic low prices.   HMW

5. Developments since last meeting

   a) HMW expressed thanks to RP for sorting out the new crockery since the last meeting.

8.05 **Sample minutes of business meeting** (continued)

6. What we have learned on courses

   RP – Confirmed that we are now accounting for management companies correctly. There have also been amendments to the related party requirements, now needing to obtain details of parents, siblings and all children.

   HMW – Recently attended a business continuity course that covered unforeseen circumstances and how to get the business going again. This didn't seem to be very relevant until an alarming accident occurred at some local estate agents' offices forcing their immediate closure. He will devise a business continuity plan in time for the next meeting.

   AS – As well as attending the same course as RP AS also reminded us of the reduction in the pension annual allowance to £50,000 from 2011/12, looking at settled purpose when discussing residency and the possible updates required to current audit letters.

   BH – Attended the same course as RP and AS.

   LS – Attended a VAT course and reminded everyone of the toolkits/ checklists available on the HMRC website.

7. Any other business

   Suggested jobs for VW next week:

   a)   Cleaning out cupboards for returning records.

   b)   Reorganising backfilling boxes to give space between letters.

   SC requested that when putting current year working papers in boxes can we ensure only six years are held (therefore removing old accounting papers if necessary).

   RP raised an issue that has occurred with Royal Mail and a recorded delivery parcel. She suggested we use the UK Mail courier instead as the costs are not too dissimilar and we know that the package will not be lost, rather than the 'don't know guv' reply she received from Royal Mail.

   RP informed us that they have located the wireless log on details.

   HMW raised the retirement party in July to be held for Mrs Jones, in the office next door and took details of attendees.

   The date of the office outing was decided as Thursday 15 September.

8. The next meeting will be held on [*day, date and time*]

The chairman asked everyone if the matters discussed had been satisfactorily dealt with.

8.06 **Tips on holding meetings**

The purposes of a meeting

1. Defines the group – who is in it
2. Revises, updates and adds to what it knows
3. Records its decision
4. Encourages commitment to decisions
5. They are the occasion when team actually exists
6. They determine hierarchy of group.

Before the meeting

1. a) Define objective (i.e. situation that needs to be discussed)
   b) What shall we do?
   c) How shall we do it?
   d) When shall we do it?
   e) Have a series of tests to see if the meeting has been a success or failure.

2. Prepare agenda
   a) Circulate to the group (over 12 is likely to be too many)
   b) Describe matters to be discussed
   c) Put agenda into order
   d) Set the time limit
   e) Don't be afraid of long agenda
   f) Head each section either 'For Information' or 'For decision'.

At the meeting, the chairman's job is to:

1. General:
   a) Start on time. Record those who attend.
   b) Encourage range of ideas.
   c) Assist and steer the meeting rather than direct it.
   d) Tell the meeting how you plan to let a complex discussion develop.
   e) Summarise what has been agreed upon.

2. The chairman's duties are:
   a) Unite the group: if a row develops let off the steam, i.e. don't let it build up. Don't take sides. Bring in the others. Stick to the facts.
   b) Focus the group: keep to the agenda. Stay alert. Keep a hand on the wheel. Test whether everyone understands the decision/remarks. Paraphrase what's been decided.
   c) Mobilise the group: protect and encourage the weak. Check round the group. Record suggestions. Build up suggestions.

After the meeting

Record the minutes
1. Time, date and place. Who is chair?
2. Names of all present and apologies
3. All agenda items – who is responsible for action
4. Main arguments leading to decision
5. Time meeting ended
6. Time, date and place of meeting.

8.07 **The art of decision making**

1. Decide what you are deciding.

   a) Is it your decision alone?

   b) Establish the limits of your responsibility.

   c) What is your decision supposed to achieve?

   d) What are the limiting factors? Cash, time?

   e) What are you really deciding about?

   f) Is the decision the right one to be focusing on? Would another decision be more effective?

2. Fix a schedule that organises the following points.

   a) Know the facts

      i) What information do I need?

      ii) Get it. Go and look, read, investigate. Ask others who've done the same.

   b) Consultation

      Involve others, particularly those concerned.

      Find out their reactions, feelings, difficulties.

3. Marginal decisions.

   a) Remind yourself of the objective.

   b) Reassess the priorities.

   c) Consider the options?

   d) Are there any other options.

   e) List pros and cons against each other.

   f) Choose whichever best meets the objectives and priorities of the situation (remember to opt for the least worst if there is no perfect decision).

   g) Sleep on the facts.

   h) Perhaps decide on no decision.

4. Brief in a group.

   Tell them:

   a) What you have decided.

   b) When the decision will take effect.

   c) Where the changes will take place.

   d) How the decision will be implemented.

   e) Who will be affected.

   f) Why you are doing it the way you have decided.

5. Check that your decision has been carried out (in detail). Have a list of those points that have to be checked.

8.08 **Decision making – tackling difficult tasks**

This template may come in handy when you are faced with a difficult decision. If you can break the problem down into its constituent elements, it might become easier.

Name: _____

Subject: _____

	Issue to be dealt with	How to be dealt with	✔
1.			
2.			
3.			
4.			
5.			
6.			
7.			

Signed: _____ Date: _____

8.09 **Template for a customer survey**

Dear_____

We are conducting a survey of our clients and we would very much value your thoughts on how you rate our product or service.

If you have the time, please answer the following questions and either post this survey back to us in the enclosed Freepost envelope or fax it to us on the number shown at the bottom. Many thanks for taking the time to do this for us.

1.   What do we get right – what do you like about our service/product?

2.   What do we get wrong – what do you dislike about our service/product?

3.   What are we not doing that you wish we would do (this is not quite the same as number 2)?

4.   How many marks out of ten would you give us?

5.   What would we have to do to score higher than this?

Signed: _____ Dated: _____

Your phone number (if you would like us to call you about your comments):

Please now either post this back to us, using the enclosed Freepost envelope, or fax it to us on 01234 567 890.

Thank you again for your time.

8.10 **Suggestions on writing a report**

A. The ten steps to report writing

1. Identify the purpose of the report and who it is being written for.
2. Assemble the information.
3. Identify relevant information.
4. Examine accuracy.
5. Evaluate the information.
6. Sort and group the information.
7. Allocate headings.
8. Write the report – there should be Contents, Headings (which should not be called 'General' or 'Misc', and they should be numbered for reference), Index (for complex documents).
9. Revision.
10. Fine-tuning.

B. Tips for report writing

1. Cut out long words and sentences.
   Fog Factor – A long word has 3 or more syllables. On any page count the long words (say 15) and divide by the number of sentences (say 5) – would give a fog factor of 3, which would be ok. A fog factor of 5 or more would be awful.
2. Be direct – i.e. clear.
3. Be brief.
4. Revise. Nobody gets it right the first time.
5. Leave time between drafts.
6. Always bear in mind the readers' requirements. ('What will they do with it?')

C. How the report should be laid out

Cover and Contents
Introductions
1. Why the report is being written
2. Who told the writer to produce the papers?
3. Limitations
4. Sources
5. Method of working
6. Objectives
7. Warning of what sort of recommendations will be made at the end
8. Caveats.
Main Body of report – divide into chunks with clear headings
Conclusion – purely for comment – no new information
Recommendations   – Action already taken.
                         – Actions to be taken.

Signature and date
Appendices, References and Index

8.11 Creating an organisation chart for your business

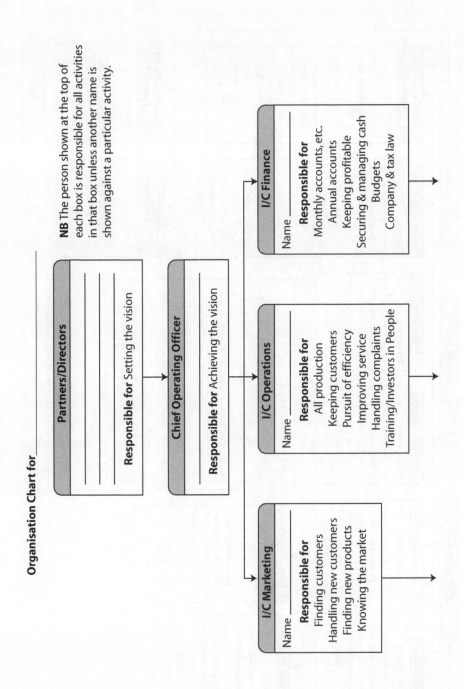

Organisation Chart for _____

NB The person shown at the top of each box is responsible for all activities in that box unless another name is shown against a particular activity.

Partners/Directors

Responsible for Setting the vision

Chief Operating Officer

Responsible for Achieving the vision

I/C Finance

Name _____

Responsible for
Monthly accounts, etc.
Annual accounts
Keeping profitable
Securing & managing cash
Budgets
Company & tax law

I/C Operations

Name _____

Responsible for
All production
Keeping customers
Pursuit of efficiency
Improving service
Handling complaints
Training/Investors in People

I/C Marketing

Name _____

Responsible for
Finding customers
Handling new customers
Finding new products
Knowing the market

continued on page 190

8.11 **Creating an organisation chart for your business** (continued)

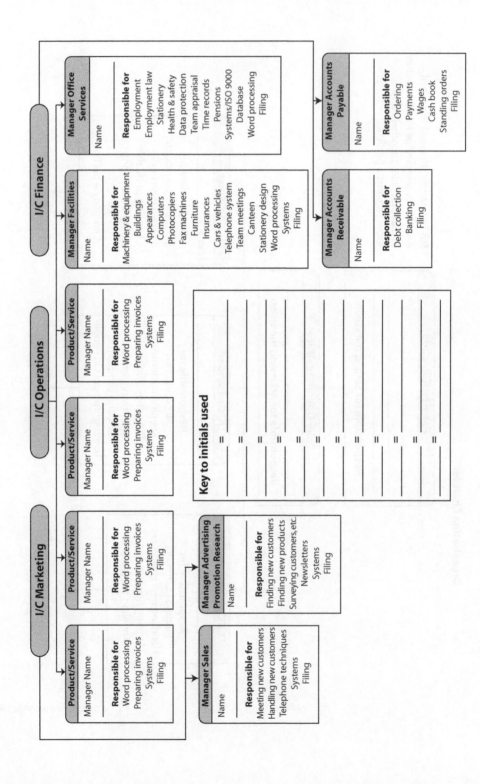

8.12 **New customer details**

Prepared by_____on_____

	Private individual	**Other – e.g. company, partnership**
Full name		
Address		
Phone		
Fax		
Mobile		
Email		
Website		
Date of birth		
Tax reference		
NI number		
Trade/business (i.e. what the business actually does)		
How did you hear about us?		
Products/Services required:		
Other		

8.13 **Suggested telephone message sheet**

FOR: _____

FROM: _____ CLIENT NO: _____

OF: _____ DATE: _____

TIME: _____

THEIR PHONE NO: _____

IN CONNECTION WITH _____

QUESTIONS ASKED/MATTERS DISCUSSED/INSTRUCTIONS GIVEN

ACTION TAKEN

FURTHER ACTION TO BE TAKEN

Signed: _____

8.14 **Suggested jobs to do list**

Jobs to do

Date_____

Urgent and quick	Done ✔	Longer jobs	Day to do	Done ✔	For later	Done ✔

8.15 **Tips on one-to-one training**

Follow this plan before beginning the training session.

- What am I going to teach?
- What are the main points for them to remember?

PLAN

1. **CONTEXT** – i.e. explain what you are going to teach and why they need to know it, where the process fits into their job and the company's business.

2. **DIGESTIBLE CHUNKS**

   a) Start by going through the process normally and then train following this invaluable maxim: 'I do it normal, I do it slow, we do it together and off you go'.

   b) Widen the session into digestible chunks (stages/key points).

   i) _____

   ii) _____

   iii) _____

   iv) _____

   v) _____

   vi) _____

   vii) _____

   viii) _____

   ix) _____

3. **PRACTICE**

   Then let them practise ('I hear and forget, I see and remember, I do* and I understand') *i.e. practise.

MATERIAL TO PREPARE BEFORE SESSION	DONE ✔
1.	
2.	
3.	
4.	

8.16 **Creating a marketing plan**

These are the elements that should go into a marketing plan:

1. [*The name of your business*]
2. Marketing plan
3. Contents

Section A – Where we are now

1. Client profile (what sort of clients do we have):

    _____

2. Product and turnover profile (what sort of products do we currently supply and how is our present turnover made up):

    _____

3. Profit profile (how profitable is each department):

    _____

Section B – Where we want to be

4. Target client profile (what would be an ideal client profile and by when):

    _____

5. Target product and turnover profile (what products (both existing and new) do we wish to supply):

    _____

Section C – The marketing action plan

6. What we plan to do to achieve:

    _____

    a) Our target client profile:

    _____

    b) Our target product profile:

    _____

    c) Our target turnover profile:

    _____

7. Who is responsible for each activity and by when:

    _____

8. Marketing ideas that we are adopting in the next 12 months:

    _____

NOTES

Index